What people are saying about

Crimson Craft

The cleverly laid out design of Quin's *Crimson Craft* ensures that not only does the reader develop an intellectual and spiritual understanding of Sex Magick as the book unfolds, but also allows the understanding of the practitioner to build with responsible foundations being laid at our feet as we step into the journey that is to come. A tantalising cocktail of academia and sexual expression as you turn each page. Beautifully and respectfully written most inclusively.

Mandi See, author of *Sex Magick – A Guide For The Modern Witch*

Suffice it to say, I needed this book! Halo Quin has the innate ability to write in such a way that I can tangibly feel their words in my body; in other words, their writing touches me. This was especially so with *Crimson Craft*, which guides readers to manifest the magic of the Red Witch through practical exercises, revealing and celebrating the Divine Erotic in the sensuality of life, and create magic! Readers are invited to embark on a healing journey, guided by the author's characteristic voice, whereby taboos are deconstructed, eros is unleashed and embraced, and Divinity is found in the sensual union of body and spirit.

Olivia Church, author of *Isis - Great of Magic, She of 10,000 Names* and *Sekhmet - Lady of Flame, Eye of Ra*

A beautiful, thoughtful and inspiring book of true magic. I loved it.

Cat Treadwell, Pagan Priestess and author of *A Druid's Tale*

Crimson Craft

Sexual magic for the solo witch

Crimson Craft

Sexual magic for the solo witch

Halo Quin

MOON
BOOKS

Winchester, UK
Washington, USA

JOHN HUNT PUBLISHING

First published by Moon Books, 2023
Moon Books is an imprint of John Hunt Publishing Ltd., No. 3 East Street, Alresford
Hampshire SO24 9EE, UK
office@jhpbooks.net
www.johnhuntpublishing.com
www.moon-books.net

For distributor details and how to order please visit the 'Ordering' section on our website.

Text copyright: Halo Quin 2022

ISBN: 978 1 78535 939 2
978 1 78535 940 8 (ebook)
Library of Congress Control Number: 2021952211

A CIP catalogue record for this book is available from the British Library.

Design: Matthew Greenfield

UK: Printed and bound by CPI Group (UK) Ltd, Croydon, CR0 4YY
Printed in North America by CPI GPS partners

We operate a distinctive and ethical publishing philosophy in
all areas of our business, from our global network of authors to
production and worldwide distribution.

Contents

Previous Titles

Your Faery Heart
(Lulu, 2010) B00932SH6U

Pixie Kisses
(Lulu, 2011) 978-1447523444

Pagan Portals – Your Faery Magic
(Moon Books, 2015) 978-1785350764

Pagan Portals – Gods and Goddesses of Wales
(Moon Books, 2019) 978-1785356216

Twisted – Honest Reflections of a Kinky Witch
(Herbary Books, 2020) 978-1916339644

All That Glitters – Wonderings & Wanderings of a Changeling Bard
(Herbary Books, 2021) 978-1916339651

Pagan Portals – Faeries, Folktales, and Spirits
(Moon Books, 2022) 978-1-78535-941-5

This book is dedicated to my Cap'n, who helped
me become a delighted bee...

To those who are where I was, seeking the sweetness
of life which you know is there...

And to Freya and the other deities of passion, who have
guided my dance upon this honeyed path.

A breath of bliss, caught upon the tongue,
I welcome you, invite you; Divine Lover, come.
Red Goddess dancing, spinning like the sun,
Wild God and Bright Spirit; come, lovers, come.
Bless my heart, my mind, my skin,
with touch of pleasure welcomed in,
in your honour I begin,
Divine Lover, come!

Crimson for passion, for lust and for love,
for the ink our tale's writ' in; our life's blood.
Crimson for the pleasure of a lover's gentle lips,
and crimson for our hearts that beat with bliss.

Preface

I am not asking you to believe...

It is likely that you picked this book up because you at least enjoy the language of magic, but belief is not a prerequisite for enjoyment of the wonders held within.

That which is magical is that which invokes a particular feeling in us, a sense of wonder and expansion that carries us beyond our ordinary understanding of things. In this sense, magic is a mood. We are enchanted when we indulge in the sensation of being part of something bigger than ourselves and it lights us up. Magic includes, to paraphrase the infamous magician Aleister Crowley, *the art of changing consciousness at will*. It is the craft of choosing which state of mind, what level of consciousness, one is in. And, for the witch, magic is being open to the possibilities beyond the explainable. Including the possibility that we can change things in our favour.

There is a saying by Arthur C. Clarke, oft repeated; *any sufficiently advanced technology is indistinguishable from magic.* Likewise, just because we have not yet explained something does not mean it will remain inexplicable. This still does not remove the magic from the world.

There is another saying; *it's all in your head, your head is just bigger than you think it is.*

I experience my gods as real. They are real to me. They are forces, encounters, experiences which seem to direct themselves. In much the same way as the wind moves independently of me. And yet, I understand them, like I understand the wind, in relation to myself and my own life. I don't need you to think of my gods as objective, supernatural beings that meddle in the world of mortals, I only invite you to encounter the experiences I name as Freya, Frey, Inanna, Eros, as experiences. As we will

1

discuss, you may think of them as personifications of magical powers, as stories which we tell ourselves about our own moods, or as archetypes dwelling in your subconscious. Or you may greet them simply as experiences, by whichever name, and see how the encounter changes you.

Perhaps for you they are poetic metaphors which describe something about the world, perhaps for you they are independent people. Or perhaps, they are both these things, and more. I do not need you to believe, I only invite you to *experience* their reality.

This is no place for shame in this work. No place for pretending that this is not real.

In this magic, we seek to become shameless and embrace the depths of love and life.

Chapter 1

Foreplay

A Warning

Dear reader, it is my firm belief that everyone can benefit from the magic offered up in this little red book, but even if that is true, this is a topic that not everyone is comfortable, or ready, to engage with. If that is you, I invite you to put this book down and make yourself a nice cup of tea instead. This is not a particularly explicit or lurid book, and there are no diagrams, but even so, if you are of a sensitive disposition around matters of a sexual nature, or a minor, then this may not be the book for you, or you may prefer to be selective about which chapters you read. I imagine, however, that as you have opened these covers it is a topic that intrigues you and so, if you're still here, we shall begin.

A Manual of Magic; How to Use this Book

This book will primarily focus on solo work and reflection, being a guidebook to solo sexual magic for healing your divinely erotic self, and conjuring your sacred power of *eros* through engaging in the world with pleasure and embodied presence.

I recommend reading and working through the book in order, but if you would prefer to explore in a different order then begin with "Part I; Casting the Circle" for the context and principles behind *Crimson Craft*. Chapter 2 explains the core energies that we will be working with, and Chapter 3 illuminates the kind of magic we will be crafting here, and what it means to be weaving this particular thread of magic.

"Part II; Laying the Foundation" includes some theory and practical pieces for your magical craft, so if you are new to witchcraft, this is essential reading, and if you have your own practice already, Chapters 4 and 5 may provide inspiration for expanding your focus, but will certainly give you an insight into the way in which your author approaches magic and witchcraft.

"Part III; Solo Erotic Magic" is where we dive into the practices, beginning with tuning into and working towards the healing of our erotic selves in Chapter 6. Chapter 7 explores the expression and communication of the erotic, as expression of ourselves is important and is in itself a magical act. Chapter 8 is where a method of spellcasting with sex magic is introduced as a method for exploring our own personal erotic power as witches and magic-users.

"Part IV; Dancing with the Gods" is where sex magic as devotion to the divine is explored, including the concepts of devotion as an expression of embodied Divine Erotic energy, the distinction between archetypes and deities, and space to begin taking your whole self into relationship. Where Chapter 9 looks at the theory and practice of devotion, Chapter 10 and 11 introduce some of the deities who are patrons of this work, for you to contemplate, or approach, as you choose.

In "Part V; Underworld Magic", Chapter 12 briefly touches on some of the more taboo aspects of sex, specifically in the connection between magical techniques and kink, or BDSM.

It is my hope that you will come away from this book with thoughts that help you find wholeness, and tools which support your journey into becoming fully present and embodied. Throughout I have included both theory and practice, as well as poetry and story-type writings, to offer alternative ways of engaging with the material.

As with any magical work, it is important to approach this with an open heart and mind, and to listen to your own intuition and instincts. You know what will be most helpful to you (as well as which things you are avoiding because they are uncomfortable, rather than risky). As you work through this material, and I will remind you of this throughout, it is important that you are kind to yourself, and get help and support if you need it.

There are both practical exercises and reflective contemplations, with questions to act as prompts to deepen your understanding and exploration of this magic. The more you engage, the more you will get out of it, but, conversely, there is no rush to do it all at once.

Checking in with yourself and Self-Love Reminders

It is a sad fact in our world that many of us have had traumatic experiences around sex and our bodies, so we need to be extra gentle on ourselves as we walk these paths to healing. Perhaps there are experiences in your past that you might need extra support around, or are not in a place to deal with at this point. Give yourself the time and leeway that you need, check-in with yourself as you go along, and tread lightly through the forest of your history. You know yourself best, so I am trusting you to look after yourself in this work. This process can take many years, it has for me, so know that there is no rush.

Spend a little time making a note of things that might be particularly challenging for you in this book. Have a look through the contents list, and maybe skim through the chapters if you like. Anywhere where you might find something particularly sensitive for you, make a note to only engage when you are in a good place to do so, in a way that is safe for you.

In each chapter I'll include a reminder to check in with yourself and engage in self-care. Even if you do not have obviously traumatic experiences, self-care is important in this work, and finding the space to show love to ourselves is part of this magic. For some of you this will be the hardest part. Do what you can and allow yourself to gently be open to showing yourself more love over time. For others, self-love is the easiest thing in the world, and I invite you to indulge yourself and to allow this to overflow into how you are in the world. What is life without a little indulgence every now and again? Each time we do this it helps us to look after ourselves better, so allow these prompts to both give you the space to ensure you are exploring this material safely for you, and to practice being good to yourself.

And please, remember to take each step at the pace you are comfortable with, many of us have challenges and wounds around these topics and magic is not therapy, even when it can assist healing. *Be kind to yourself* and trust that you are on the right path, and there is no need to push yourself harder or faster than is healthy for you. Or indeed to engage with any aspect which would not be safe for you to engage with.

SSC & Ethics

Alongside the importance of self-care, I would like to highlight something important in anything relating to sex; consent, ethics and safety.

There is a concept which was codified over recent decades in kinky communities and which is just as important within a magical practice. Though the language is ever evolving, it can be expressed through the watchwords of *Safe, Sane, and Consensual*, often abbreviated to *SSC*.

Sex is complex. And it is absolutely possible to misuse and abuse it, but that does not make it inherently bad in itself. This is why consent is so important. The kinky cornerstones of *Safe, Sane, and Consensual* are foundational to healthy sexual expression. It means; engage in ways that minimise risk and make it as safe as you can, care for your mental health and try to ensure that everyone is in a good place for both safety and are able to consent, and ensure that everyone involved is honestly, freely, and happily consenting from a place of being informed. Once these aspects are in place sexual expression can range from gentle playfulness to serious ritual and everything in between.

Ethics can also mean asking questions of ourselves about how we support the creators of work which offers us value and healing in our lives, from writing to art, images and videos. If you engage with erotica or porn, for example, do you know that the creators and performers are being supported and looked after? Are you supporting the creators in getting paid to survive? If you enjoy their work, or believe it should be available, are you willing to speak up for sex workers when they come under attack? These are all questions to ask yourself over time, to develop one's own integrity and ability to work effective magic.

Ethics are essential to a healthy magical practice. The Witch does not need to follow someone else's moral code; they live by their own ethics, in integrity and alignment with their best self and allowing others to be in integrity and alignment themselves. And, if we are honouring love, sex, healing, pleasure, and the magic of *eros*, then behaving ethically towards and around others is a part of this too.

I invite you, now, to take a moment and reflect on your ethics. What values are important to you? What is your personal ethical code? How do you expect to be treated by others, and how would you expect to treat them? What do you think of the concept of "Safe, Sane, and Consensual" as guidelines for practice? More modern versions of SSC include "Risk-Aware", "Informed" and "Personal Responsibility" but the thread that runs through all of these is "consensual". What thoughts do you have around the concepts of risk-awareness and personal responsibility?

Crafting your Crimson Grimoire

Books are magical. They contain thoughts made manifest; magic made tangible. Books can offer a foundation to build upon, and your own book of magic is no exception. This is the first magical tool I recommend that you create, and by the end it will contain the spells and prayers that work for you.

The magical journal that you use while working with the material in this book will become your Crimson Grimoire; a spell book and magical record of *your* path through the Crimson Craft.

If you do not already have a magical journal then your first task is to acquire a blank book, paper, or a digital folder in which to contain records of the magic that you do, the prayers and spells that you try, and the results. Your personal grimoire can contain anything magical that you find useful as well as your experiences.

I highly recommend keeping notes on your understanding and experiences of magic, your dreams, your workings, and the outcomes. You may wish to develop a shorthand to obscure that which you write if you are concerned about prying eyes, but something that will remind you of your journey is invaluable. It allows you to look back and see how far you've come, what worked and what didn't, and what you've learned but then forgotten. In a world full of information, keeping a note of the pieces you glean from your practice allows you to hold onto it for longer, and means you can remind yourself of the evidence you have gathered if, or when, doubts seep in.

You may want to put your grimoire together in a ring binder or folder, or in a book which you leave blank pages at the start for a table of contents. Record prayers, spells, and charms that you love. Note down oracle readings, connections you notice, deities and myths that you encounter which resonate for you. Quotes, poetry, rituals, images, symbols, correspondences... include it all. Let this be your working book, and take note of the pages you return to for reference over and over. These hold the keys to the practices that matter most to you.

I have a shelf of magical journals and returning to them at important moments really helps me to see how I have evolved, and to remind myself of tools that helped me, ideas that I've developed, and wisdom that I've heard from others over the years. Magic is both an art and a science. An art because it is important to work through intuition and to weave the sensual beauty that speaks to your soul into what you are doing, and a science because every magical working is an experiment. This means you start with a hypothesis; you test it through your working, and you check to see if the results match the goal. If it works perfectly, notes help you to replicate the spell or working when you need those results in the future. If it doesn't work, or doesn't quite come out the way you'd hoped, then you can check your notes to see what might need changing next time, or what you changed that made it better or worse than previously.

I like to start my grimoires and journals with a book blessing on the first page, so I offer this one to you to use in yours, or as inspiration for writing your own inside the book or folder which you choose to be your Crimson Grimoire;

I declare this book a blessed work of Arte,
A tome to hold safe the magic of my heart,
Within its pages let me map my way,
And conjure love and eros, through the night and day.
Keep its secrets safe from prying eyes
And bless my work and play, in this crafting of the wise.

Allow me to introduce myself...

Sex is so personal, so powerful, and so important that here, more than with any other strand of magic, it may help for you to know a bit about me and my background so that you can hear my words in context as we navigate some challenging topics within these pages.

I am known as Halo, or Ms Quin, and my deepest magical roots are in Feri Witchcraft and Reclaiming, both queer, sex positive, traditions, with a strong thread of healing the split between flesh and spirit that our culture has encouraged. I'm a practicing pagan, a witch, and a druid, with relationships with various deities, and a lifelong love-affair with the Fae. I've taught ceremonial magic as well as "low magic". I trained as a holistic therapist in my teens, and a philosopher in my 20s with a particular interest in embodied experience. I've practiced storytelling, dancing, painting, poetry... and the thing these all have in common, for me, is that they are all about bringing the beauty and magic of spirit into manifest, embodied expression.

Overcoming the false dichotomy, that binary model that divides body and soul and drags us away from living with delight, from holding our own personal power in our own hands, is central to what I do.

Most of my experience of the world is as someone who is seen as female. Which means I've had the usual messages of objectification, of being judged for being "sexual" (when I was just being present) or "frigid" (when I was enforcing my boundaries), and of being denied the value of pleasure. Gender is something that has always confused me, however, and here too the binary so prevalent in our culture makes little sense to me as a hard rule. But I recognise that there are experiences that shape my understanding of the world and how others see me. And again, this binary model of gender is, while useful to some, not my experience of myself or, ultimately, of the Divine.

So, I am a non-binary, queer, woman. A magician, and a witch.

About Gender, Polarity, and Language

Because I could see how important gender is to so many people (whether they are cis, trans, or otherwise) I spent many years working to get to grips with "divine feminine" and "divine masculine" energies. What are they? How are they different? Where do they play a role? The conclusion I came to was that, yes, there are feminine and masculine energies, just as there are various queer energies, and that these are just that; part of a spectrum of energies. Following the Tantric tradition, and the influence of Carl Jung and others, many books on sex magic discuss the balancing and union of masculine and feminine energies with one's partner (or within oneself). Working with the tension between them and the union of them is one model of sex magic, but it is not what this book is focused on. There is gendered language in this book, both binary and non-binary, but this is as part of the multifaceted expression of experience and I ask that you read it within the spirit of understanding that this is a fluid, inclusive model. All are welcome in this work, binary and non-binary, cis and trans, and regardless of ethnicity, race, or sexual orientation. Finally, language and cultural understanding is constantly changing so I have done my best to hold an inclusive space in the terms I've used, but if I have gotten it wrong, or if language has changed over time, then please accept my work in the spirit with which it is written.

If this is something which confuses or intrigues you, then have a look in the Further Reading Appendix for suggestions as to where you can explore more about gender in magic.

And now, let us begin...

Part I
Casting the Circle

Chapter 2

The Divine Erotic

A Vision; Dance of the Divine Erotic

A Goddess holds out Her arms.
She is surrounded by warmth and darkness, firelight and softness, and the bright glinting of flame on cold stone. Her robes are deep blood red and swirl around her like they are alive.

A God holds out His arms.
He is tall and in the shadows above his head it appears that he wears horns which reach up to the sky. Deep green smoke flows about him as he smiles at you.

A Divine Spirit holds out Their arms.
Blue and white and brightly shining, they hold the edge and welcome you in. Their presence is shifting and clear all at once. You know that there is a home for you here in their dance.

We live our lives on the edges of possibility. Our day to day of existence passing like a river as we ride the ride of life.

Life. That gift we so often take for granted. That divine spark which fills us in every moment until our death.

We are here, now, alive. And every breath contains the possibility for romancing life, for weaving magic into every cell and sinew, and for living with all we have to live. Remember the pleasure in inhaling a beautifully scented flower. Think of the delight in a soft caress. Imagine the last glorious sunset you saw, all the colours that heralded the coming of night and took your breath away. The music that conjures dancing in your fingers and toes. The tastes that make you purr with pleasure. The things that fill your heart with beauty and delight. The touch of a lover. The ecstasy of orgasm. The bliss of relaxation. These are sensual, erotic pleasures that remind us that we are alive. These are divinely erotic moments which offer us connection, power, and magic.

When these things are met with innocent, honest, delight, and allowed to carry us into our highest potential, there we meet the Divine. There we meet the gods of sex, love, and magic. The deities of passion and The Divine Erotic within ourselves. In this meeting we begin to heal the wounds caused by the denial of this part of ourselves.

An Invocation

Witchcraft, as craft, is a practice in which we invoke and conjure the magic which we are working with. One of the simplest acts of magic we can perform is a prayer to call on the energies we are seeking to cultivate, and so I invite you now to find a safe and comfortable space, and to light a candle, and to read the following aloud, with feeling;

A breath of bliss, caught upon the tongue,
I welcome you, invite you; Divine Lover, come.
Red Goddess dancing, spinning like the sun,
Wild God and Bright Spirit; come, lovers, come.
Bless my heart, my mind, my skin,
with touch of pleasure welcomed in,
in your honour I begin,
Divine Lover, come!

Sit for a while and just notice how you feel, how the atmosphere has changed, and any impressions you may receive.

Later, you may repeat this and choose to journal in your grimoire, or perform some divination if that is part of your practice, but for now, just be with the experience.

When you are ready, take a breath into your belly, and read aloud the following, with gratitude;

Lovers three I honour you,
Let your blessings flow,
Know that you are welcome here,
and help my magic grow.
Let me know your sacred ways,
Of love and sex divine,
For now I bid you kind farewell,
You to your homes and me to mine.

Extinguish the candle safely, make any notes you'd like to, and let the experience settle in you for a moment before going to do something grounding and mundane to bring you back to the everyday world.

What is the Divine Erotic?

The Divine Erotic, or *eros*, is the energy of being alive and embodied. It is that thrill of pleasure in beauty and the drive of healthy desire. We find it most clearly in sexual desire and sexual pleasure, but this is only one aspect of it.

Pleasure itself is powerful. It shows us where we are engaged in being embodied, being present in the world and open to life. Our sensual being delights in pleasure. Our bodies, hearts, and spirits sing with joy when we allow ourselves to enjoy being alive in the world. When our needs are met and we are safe, then we can do things which feel good because they are good for us.

There is a distinction between destructive, unhealthy pleasures, and the healthy pleasure of embodied delight. Know that when I speak of pleasure I am not speaking of the former, but of that which truly honours our existence as divine beings living as part of the earthly realm. This is the divine erotic power of sensual pleasure. The energy of positive passion and desire, not as greed but as a lust for life, is lifeforce flowing freely through us and, as living beings, this is a good thing. It awakens our spirits and soothes our hearts, allowing us to connect with other beings in healthy ways.

Eros is also that power as it manifests in the world around us and is expressed through archetypes and deities who can reflect back to us aspects of ourselves and guide us in reclaiming that which we have lost.

Throughout this book we will be guided by the Divine Erotic in several ways. We will explore how it manifests within the Witch themselves, and through magic, to begin to bring us back home to ourselves and strengthen our core magical selves. Then we will step into the circle with the deities of passion who manifest *eros*, sacred sexual energy, and explore the devotional aspect of being in relationship with this energy and these powers. As we near the end of this journey we will touch on some of the darker elements of sexual magic, and consider the magic of the erotic in the underworld of the dungeon. In this way we will traverse the three realms; the middle world where we live, the upper world of the gods, and the lower world of the subterranean powers. Finally, we will end with a ritual to integrate the work we've been doing and to each choose our path ahead.

A Reflection

Take up your magical journal and spend a while in contemplation:

What does the idea of "the Divine Erotic" conjure for you?
Does consensual, sensual pleasure feel sacred to you?
Do you feel like eroticism could be sacred too?

Eros

In Ancient Greece, "*eros*" was the primordial power of love and desire, who was said to have joined with the primordial Chaos to give life to the whole human race. A little later, *eros* because personified as the companion, or son, of Aphrodite, "Eros", and eventually he was remembered as the lover of Psyche; The Soul, and as the father of Pleasure.

The energy of "*eros*" was also passionate, sexual, love, the root of our word "erotic", and a powerful force in its own right. For clarity; in this book I will indicate that I am talking about "*eros*" as this magical, sensual energy with italics, and the occasional reference to "Eros" as a deity, will be unitalicized.

From this we can see that the force of *eros* was understood as not just pleasure, but the foundation of life. *Eros*, as deity or power, was described as core to the existence of humanity. This plays out in our lives; in the best cases desire shows us what we must move towards and passion is the fire that moves us, and every individual life is created through a process where pleasure and desire are built in to the mechanics, and, hopefully, the actuality of it.

As life-creating desire *eros* is a force of bringing together, of union, of manifestation, and of pleasure. In life we can feel erotic pleasure both in the act of being manifestly alive, and of coming together within ourselves, or with others, in pleasure. In this Craft, *eros* as power is another name for the erotic-made-divine, and thus is erotic love. Physical pleasure raised to the power of deity, where spirit and flesh meet.

Eros is the power channelled in sex magic and honoured in the path of the Red Witch.

Practical: Tuning into *Eros*

Eros is an energy available to all of us. It is part of who and what we are, and is as much a part of us as our breath. Indeed, you can experience this magic right now.

Allow yourself to be comfortable.
Take a deep breath and gather yourself, and as you breathe out, allow your body to relax.

Allow your bones to support you upon the earth.

Allow your spirit to settle in your belly and your heart.

Allow your breath to fill you and soothe you.

And as you breathe, begin to notice the tingle on your skin.

Begin to notice the gentle charge of magic like a song or spark or glow in your heart.

Notice it in your belly.

Notice it in your genitals.

Notice that magic in your body growing and glowing with each breath.

Feel that power, that energy of eros, of embodied pleasure and magic, in your self.

Know that this is yours.

This power is your power.

This magic is your magic.

It is part of the witch-power that you can choose to draw on, to conjure change and enchant your life.

Stay with this feeling for a little while.

When you are ready, take one final deep breath and as you breath out release this feeling, allowing the magic to sink into your bones and bless you with eros; the pleasure of magic, the divine erotic power which is your birth right.

Follow me to the temple

Follow me to the temple
where we can dance once again
Follow me to the temple
of the goddess of pleasure and pain.

Meet me now in the circle
of arms holding each other tight,
meet me now in the circle
where we make each other feel right.

Light the bright flame of passion
so I can look in your eyes
light the bright flame of passion
and tell me what you desire.

Break the chains of old stories
the cages that long kept us small
break the chains of old stories
it is all we have to stand tall.

Say yes to the kissing of life,
and the limits and love of the flesh
say yes to the kissing of life
and let yourself make a wish.

Follow me to the temple
where we can dance once again
follow me now to the temple
of the goddess of pleasure and pain.

Self-Love Check-In

How are you feeling about this so far? Has anything made you uncomfortable that you might need to be gentle with yourself around? Is there anything that really excited you? Is there anything that felt like coming home?

Take a moment now to make a list of three things:

1. One thing you can do right now that will be good for you. Perhaps you need a glass of water, or a movement break. Perhaps sending a message to a loved one would feel good. Maybe you need some food.

2. One thing that takes 5-15 minutes that would make you smile now. Perhaps putting on your favourite song, or playing a game, or going outside and watching the birds, clouds, stars, or sunset. Perhaps cuddling your favourite person or stuffed toy, putting on an item of clothing or jewellery that makes you feel cosy, or reading a favourite poem.

3. One thing you are grateful for right now.

Look over your list. Now, or as soon as you can, go and do the first two items on it.

Chapter 3

Red Witchcraft

The Red Witch

The Witch sinks into their body, rooting deeply in the power of the flesh, which is, truly, tangible spirit. In this culture, we are encouraged away from connecting with our bodies, we are taught to view them from the outside, we are told that they do not belong to us. We are taught that only certain forms of love or desire are acceptable, we are taught to deny and repress our natural drives. We are rarely taught how to express them in healthy ways. We are split from our flesh, stripped of our power, and domesticated...

The Witch is one who chooses to be feral. Embodied. To reach out for that wild magic and dance with it. In our world we are taught to *sit still* to *behave* to *conform*. We are taught that we do not have a choice over our bodies, that we do not have power over our expression, that we exist for the business owners who pay us, the exam board who judge us, the people who watch us.

The Witch takes back ownership of their body, and the strength that comes with it. Today so many of us have had our lives controlled by others, and so many have had our bodies used by those with more worldly power than us – social, financial, physical. Our bodies hurt and we often do not know how to heal them, so we retreat further from the flesh. If it does not matter then they cannot hurt us with it. When we do this, we give away our power. Our magic. Our birth right.

The Witch chooses healing. It is not an easy path. But it is one that is full of magic, of wonder, and of pleasure. In the modern Western world, those who embrace the term "Witch" have often distanced our Craft from aspects of life which might get us further misunderstood by popular culture. For many, witchcraft today is a private spiritual practice, a religious path, but, being unusual, it often gets mistaken for something *wicked*. To encourage acceptance, those that practice witchcraft often minimise the role of things like sexual power in magic, as sex is so often considered something shameful. We sanitize our image for the tastes of others. This is a protective measure, to present our practice as palatable and acceptable. But it also further cuts us off from our power. The power in our flesh and bones and blood. The power of being alive, whole, embodied.

Conformity is not inherently negative, when it is a genuine choice that helps us and those we care about, but it can be hard to recognise when we are conforming for the sake of conformity, or out of fear, and denying our own strength or sacrificing our own health. This kind of conformity for the sake of conformity is worth avoiding, or using consciously as a tool, rather than as a default. Knowledge, here as in all things, truly is power. Choosing wholeness and authenticity, is magic.

You may have heard of colour-coded witches before. It is a popular thing to claim to be a "white witch", who "does no harm", or a "green witch" who loves the trees... I dislike limiting magic by colour-coding the craft as these are not restraints but only descriptive, and it is easy to forget that the label is not the whole truth, but it does give you a symbol to hold onto, a picture to remember. The *Red Witch* is one who does not shirk from claiming their power just because sex is a touchy subject in polite company. A Red Witch is willing to explore the true and healthy desires of their own bodies, their own hearts. We are working towards being whole human beings, magical bones and all. A Red Witch, then, is a Witch for whom the body, passion, and pleasure are sacred. Not owed to or from anyone else, and not to be denied.

A Reflection

Take up your magical journal and consider these thoughts:

How embodied do you feel?

How in tune with your body are you?

What is your relationship with your body like?

How do you feel about the word "witch"?

How does the thought of being seen as "wicked" for having personal power make you feel?

In what ways do you conform, and in what ways do you rebel? And how often is the conformity or rebellion coming from a place of authenticity?

Sacred Sex

Sex is sacred. There is no division between flesh and spirit but that which is in our language. We conceptualise a separation which keeps us from the power which rides through our body, the magic which is known in ecstasy.

The earth is only one layer of existence, one manifestation of spirit, one vibration of energy. The flesh is spirit in its most tangible step in the dance of life, not a distinct thing, but a phase of expression. Just as ice is the same substance as water and steam, so too is the physical the same substance as the spiritual; we are life standing here in many states all at once.

So, when I say that sex is sacred, I mean not that it is something which is only meant for more "spiritual" folk, no. I mean that the body is holy, we are spirit walking the earth, and the pleasure found when we are fully present in healthy sexual expression is divine.

Sex is not limited to intercourse, nor is it attraction. Sex includes those things for many of us, but sex is so much more than simple fucking. Simple fucking, however, is definitely sex, definitely as holy as any other aspect of our physical existence, and definitely worthy of honouring, if that is part of your life.

25

If it is not, that is also ok. Pleasure and sensual embodiment, sex as desire, connection, and lifeforce, is not dependent on intercourse. And even sexual pleasure is not dependent on another person. The Divine Erotic is for every human to find in themselves and the world, in the form that works for them. It is pleasure in being alive, being embodied, and the magic and power that comes with that.

As sex is sacred it is never owed to another, and never required. As something sacred it is to be treated with respect and never forced upon another or used for harm. Sexual acts are expressions of *eros*, ways of reaching for our ecstatic magic and to connect with the Divine Lover. Acts which look like sex but are done to subvert that connection are not about this at all. Approach each act of sex, of eroticism, of pleasure, as though you are touching the Divine, and you will.

All acts of love and pleasure are my rituals.
~ *The Charge of the Goddess (Doreen Valiente)*

Sex Magic

Sex Magic has more than one purpose, more than one manifestation, including:

~ Sexual Healing
~ Raising Power to conjure and cast spells
~ Uniting with the Divine

All three are discussed in this book. Where you go after that is between you and the Magic.

A Reflection

Take up your magical journal and contemplate the questions below.

Why did you pick up this book?
What interests you about sex magic?
What is your experience with working with sex magic before? Or
with eros and the deities of passion?

Story; An Initiation

Each word a kiss of magic,
Weaving holy spells
Of ink and breath and longing
As thunderous desire swells

I am wandering through the forest, my path lit with a single thread to guide me from the darkness. I feel the pulling in my belly as I step, step, step, along the rough dirt track towards... I do not know. I walk for a long time. I have been walking for a longer time. The drumming of the forest resonates in my bones and summons life yet. I begin to dance.

My bones have felt the chains
The cage that kept me small
I picked the lock and danced the edge
To fly first I must fall...

A clearing opens ahead, the deep red moon above, full, drips its light across the glade, marking out in shadows a waiting circle of figures with space for just one more. The two nearest me hold out their hands to mine and I join them, closing the circuit. The glimmering moon meets shimmering fire, smoke weaving through my hair and bringing me back to the night I felt the god of poets fill me, the night I felt the hand of the witch-queen, my Goddess, wrap itself undeniably around my heart.

She holds me
The hand of Love
My roots run deep
To Her stars above...

In the smoke two dancers writhe, they meld and merge and sometimes it seems there is only one. Sometimes it seems there are three. The hands gripping mine hold tight and a rolling, wordless chant begins, sounds of the forest and the soil, of the full-moon-light that bathes us, of the land beneath. It breathes through my lungs and lifting my spirit out of my flesh and carrying us all up above the canopy, up into the sky, bodies far below. My companions and I fly, far above the world, and I hear a voice telling me;

Go Back.

The stars sing with heavenly music and I want nothing more than to lose my cares in their light but still the darkness whispers;

Go Back.

My companions move like they know the way and I suppose that I do too, if I allow myself to admit it.

Go Back.

One by one they hesitate, slowing. They hear the command too.

Go Back.

It becomes more insistent and yet, and yet it never once says why. My resolve is set. I call out;

*I cannot go back, I will not, I have come for more
than this, and I will have it.*

The voice of the darkness chuckles, tenderly, softly. Full of love.

Then for the love of all that is holy, do not let go.

We begin to spin, holding each other tight, and the music of
the stars flows into us, into me. I feel myself expand, growing
brighter as we dance the dance of the heavens until we should
be tired, and yet it has only been a moment. Time has ceased
to mean anything. And... I miss it. I miss the kiss of the wind
on my cheek, the scent of smoke in my hair, the rough ground
underfoot and the warmth of the fire. As I remember these
things, I feel my body calling me. Far below the fire is burning
down. My companions feel it too. I sink. Some of us resist at
first, but together, we sink, slow, but moving faster as resistance
is released. Then I realize; we are leading each other *home*. The
voice in the darkness smiles.

I am still chanting the wordless chant but it is different now,
woven into the familiar sounds of the earth are melodies of
heaven. My hands grip those of my companions tight and we
slowly let go. The dancers are still dancing, two, three, one. I
feel it when the last member of our circle finds their feet on
the dirt again and we begin to stamp our feet in time with the
starlit music that spills from us. We begin to dance the dance of
the stars on the earth. The first dancers move to the edge of the
glade, spinning around the circle as we move inward, drawing
towards the centre.

The pulse of the earth rises up through my feet as the song of
the stars winds down through my crown. The twinned powers
fill me as I move, cares gone.

In this circle, bathed in moonlight, filled with the light of the
moon and the stars, the strength of the earth in my bones, I am

home. Later, when I leave the glade, I shine so brightly that I need no other light to find my way, but I am no longer lost on the path, I am on a journey, still unfolding.

Self-Love Check-In

How are you doing? Has anything excited or unsettled you in this chapter? What might that tell you about yourself? How do you feel about the idea that embodiment can help with magical work? Is the idea of working towards feeling more comfortable in your body an exciting one? How comfortable are you with the idea of sex being sacred? Is there anything you need to do to support yourself in working towards a better relationship to these concepts?

Take a few minutes to check in with yourself and make a list of three things, as we did in Chapter 2.

1. What do you need right now?
2. What do you desire?
3. What are you grateful for?

Go and do at least one thing you need and one thing you desire. Look after yourself and allow yourself to experience pleasure.

Part II
Laying the Foundation

Chapter 4

The Craft of the Witch

A practice of Magic

Witchcraft is a practice of magic which is rooted deeply in the body, the land, the manifest realm. It is so easy to ignore our bodies, to disappear into mental pursuits and to value the mind over the body, but where does the mind find its roots? Many religious paths place the body at the bottom of the hierarchy, a necessary evil to be endured and cast aside in favour of a nebulous soul. But what if the body is as much a part of the soul as any other part of you? Let's play a game, a wondering game, that opens us with curiosity toward moving past this split from ourselves.

What if...

What if the division between spirit and flesh, or mind and matter, is entirely arbitrary? What if that division is taught precisely because it cuts us off from the most direct route to power that we have? If we value the mental or spiritual, the intangible, and dismiss the body as merely a vessel, how can we find the power in it?

Take a moment to remember when you felt like the world might be magical, whatever that means to you. When you felt your own power. When you felt most alive. I'll bet that it was when you were *feeling* something. *Being present* in your body and self.

The converse of this is that when we begin exploring embodied, magical, practices we may find that we are tapping into more energy, more feeling, more information than we are used to, and that can take time and practice to learn how to manage it safely. When the mind, body, and spirit move in sync, each has access to the power normally held by the others and so needs to be strong enough to carry that new influx.

Think of it like this: a vessel carrying water may be fine when only half filled. Perhaps it has been knocked or cracked, but the damaged areas are still strong enough to cope with the pressure of half the amount of water it can carry, especially if the water is only moving gently. But when more water is poured in the pressure increases and the cracks may begin to leak. We are the vessel, and magic is the water. We are used to the amount we normally carry, whatever that is for us, so adding more can highlight or aggravate old mental, emotional, spiritual, and physical damage. This can be a really good thing if we take note and use the opportunity to gently heal those cracks, and if we have the support and resources to do so. So, build up slowly. Take your time and allow yourself to be aware of what is possible. And be gentle on yourself if things do get uncomfortable. Watch for leaks and engage in mending them as you go. Trust me, it's worth it.

A Reflection

Take up your magical journal and contemplate the questions below.

When have you felt most alive?
When have you felt powerful in yourself?
What might it be like to find magic in embodied living?

The Cost of Magic

The cost of magic
of following its call
of dancing down the path it carves
through your heart
your bones
your flesh
of opening to the possibility
of possibility...
The cost of magic,
for every moment of ecstasy
granted by the kiss of spirits
and the song of the storm
and the growing into
more than you could ever dream of being...
The price asked,
owed,
taken,
for the wonders gifted
over and over and over and over
for the flash of green
and feasts that last forever
for the wild flight
and gentle caress of glamour...
the cost of surrender
of saying yes
of magic...
is your life fully lived.

Practicalities First

Witchcraft gives us constant opportunities to grow, to expand our abilities, and so the practice of magic can be a constant invitation to face old wounds and choose to heal them. Know that this is always your choice, however, and you do not have to face everything right now. Our bodies hold the memories of all we have lived through, and some of us have lived through quite painful things. We might need support to heal, or release, some things. If you encounter something like that in yourself, I invite you to consider what kind of support might be the right choice for you and to seek it out when you are ready.

A witch is nothing if not practical; use the tools available to you and take the steps that are right for you. Amend, adapt, and flow with what is right and possible for you now. Beginning to come to terms with the fact that we are, culturally, severed from our bodily power and that that is something we can choose to reclaim when we are ready, is one big way we can begin to reclaim the power of the flesh.

For this reason, I would like to offer some foundational magical practices, for those that may find them useful.

Tools of the Craft

Witchcraft is the term we apply to what was historically the purview of those who struggled in society. The majority of our magical ancestors would not have claimed that term for themselves, but today, here, it has been claimed as a symbol of rebellion against the cultural norms that seek to strip our power away from us. As such, it should require very little money or material power. At the heart of witchcraft is relationship; relationship with the spirits, with the magic of the world, and with your own self. Which means that you need very few tools to practice witchcraft.

The most powerful tools you have are your body, your mind, and your spirit. Yes, including if you are disabled in some way.

Many witches are disabled, perhaps some of us pursue this path because our limitations in navigating the material realm in more commonly accepted ways leave us looking for other ways to survive and thrive. Perhaps because we already have a different, outsiders' perspective. Regardless of the reason, witchcraft is by definition accessible.

One powerful tool for the witch is visualisation, but this term is not restricted to the visual. Wherever someone refers to visualisation, or using your imagination, remember that this includes all the senses. Our imagination is powerful, and it is how we direct energy. So, when we visualise, or imagine that we feel, hear, or otherwise sense, the magic moving in the direction we are intending for it, we are shaping and directing the energetic world around us. Personally, I have a strong visual imagination, but that is not how I experience magic. I *feel* it instead. Allow your strengths to shine through in your approach and trust in yourself. You'll soon notice the results.

Soon, I'll suggest some ways in which you can begin tuning into and strengthening your personal power. Along the way I'll mention materials which you might find useful in enhancing your magic. If you do not have them, or cannot get them easily, then adapt. Use what you have already.

With that in mind, some items you may wish to begin gathering;

Candles

Candles can be of any kind, but be sure that you are keeping fire-safety in mind. Ensure you have secure holders, light them away from soft furnishings, never leave them unattended, and have something to put out accidental fires nearby. You can use different types of candles;

~ Taper candles are best for short meditations as you can light them for five minutes at a time repeatedly.

~ Tea-lights are best burnt entirely in one or two sittings.
~ Birthday candles are fine for very short spell-workings, but be careful as the holders that come with them will melt.
~ Beeswax candles are lovely, but burn hotter than paraffin, so be extra careful with the melted wax.

If you're using a candle, make sure you also have candle-lighting materials to hand. Alternatives to candles include; oil lamps, incense cones with fiery scents like cinnamon, battery powered candles, a white or fire coloured pebble or piece of card with a symbol for fire drawn upon it.

Salt

Salt is really useful for cleansing. You can just use table salt, or you can get sea salt, rock salt, or kosher salt. Entirely your choice. You can have a special container to keep it in, or you can just shake some out of the kitchen cupboard when required. I recommend not dipping tools into the salt you're going to put on your chips later though.

A Mirror

Some of the practices in this book involve a mirror, to allow you to look at yourself from the outside. You can use any mirror you can take into your ritual space; it needn't be specially dedicated to magic at all. I recommend that you cleanse it before use however, to clear away any negative impressions of yourself that you've draped over it, and to clean any marks away so that you can get a clearer view. Wiping it down with salt water or white vinegar is enough, or even just whatever you would usually use to clean it with, plus the intent to clear away any energetic dirt that might get in the way. If you are blind this might seem like a pointless tool but you can also use the mirror to reflect yourself back to yourself energetically. If you haven't experimented with that you might like to explore that aspect. Alternatively, recording tools such as a dictaphone or voice recorder (on your phone, for example) can be used to explore audio "reflections" of yourself.

Incense

Incense is wonderful for clearing and shifting energy in a space, for creating atmosphere, and for inviting in specific energies. If you can have smoke in your space (and are comfortable with it) then incense sticks of cones are a good place to begin. You can use a traditionally magical scent such as sandalwood (synthetic sandalwood is best as the wood itself is endangered now) or frankincense. Rose, cinnamon, and musk are all associated with sex and love magic. You can use your favourite scents or experiment with these, or others that appeal. If you get the opportunity to smell different scents and test out which one best conjures the feeling you are looking for for you then that is ideal. Once you've found one or two that work best, stick with those so that the association becomes stronger, and soon all you'll need to do to get into the right mindset for this work is to light the incense that you have chosen.

If you cannot use smoke then essential oils, in an oil burner, dripped into hot water and allowed to evaporate, or on fabric which you lay out or waft around your space, wax melts, or room fragrance reeds are also good ways of employing scent.

Scent ties in strongly with our memories and, if you can include it in your magic, can be a powerful tool for shifting your consciousness and conjuring *eros*.

Images or Items Representing The Power of Eros

It can be helpful to gather images or objects which remind you of the Divine Erotic which you are tuning into. Deity images, or items associated with them can help to remind you that they are nearby, as can images that feel like *eros* to you. Red is a colour that works for a lot of people, as the colour of passion, courage, sex and love. Pink and white may feel good to you to include, especially if you feel the need to remind yourself of love and the sacredness of sexual magic. Find a place to keep these objects, whether on a shelf, or in a box or bag which you can open and set out the contents when you are doing this work. In Chapter 6 we will create a shrine, where you set your reminders and create a physical home for this magic in your life, but you might choose to begin this process now.

Begin to explore music, poetry, and writings that feel like *eros* too. You might create a quote-book or playlists of your favourite sex-magic songs, the ones that feel erotic, remind you of love, or make you feel gorgeous in yourself.

As you gather your material, consider the sources. Ensure that whatever you are collecting has been created and shared consensually, following the *Safe, Sane, and Consensual* guidelines outlined in the forward. Here, as always, employ your sense of what is ethical, especially regarding imagery.

Comfort and Support

Pull out your journal and make a list of the sources of comfort and support in your life. Alongside each item on your list, include what they are good at supporting you with. This list might include friends you can phone for company at short notice, people who are better at practical things, or those that are great at distracting you with humour. You might list services you have access to, such as your local counsellors, or a massage therapist. You might include your favourite places to walk or sit, or comfort foods, music, stories, and objects. Leave space to add to your list as time goes on. Refer to this list when you need to. Asking for help and allowing yourself to be cared for when you need to, and caring for yourself in ways that help you, are important pieces of the work of the witch.

An Oracle

As someone who is working with the unseen realm, with spirits (such as deities, ancestral spirits, or spirits of the land), and with the subconscious parts of yourself, you may well find it useful to have a method of communicating intuitively with those beings and archetypes. You may already have one, or several, oracles which you already work with, but if not; Tarot, runes, ogham, oracle decks, pendulums, the I Ching, tea leaf reading, and so on are all time-honoured methods. So are divining by playing cards, by seeking synchronicity in the songs played on the radio or the signs in the world around you, and by scrying in water, fire, smoke, clouds, and so on. The method you choose does not need to be expensive, it only needs to work for you. If you do not already have a preferred divination system, I would recommend investigating oracle decks as they are often the most straightforward to read, and have the broadest range of themes and art. As such they are often a good place to find art and imagery that speak to you. If runes or ogham appeal you can make yourself a set on lollipop sticks, or on wood or pebbles you find or gather, or even simply blank index cards. Even if you have an oracle already you may find that you want to keep one specifically for your work with the crimson side of the craft. Trust your intuition on this.

Once you have your chosen oracle you can begin to incorporate it into your magical practice in various ways.

~   Daily single card/rune/symbol readings.
~   A single or three piece reading on whatever piece of information or question you are contemplating, alongside your journaling.
~   When you find yourself stuck or confused; divination.
~   When speaking to your guides, pull a card for their response.
~   Play with your oracle and get to know it.

Sex Toys

Perhaps you already own some sex toys, perhaps you do not. Equally, whether or not you choose to use them in this work is a personal decision, and both options are entirely valid. If you do choose to use sex toys, you may decide to dedicate one specifically to this work of sexual healing and erotic magic, or you may simply use your usual, favourite toys. It is worth considering whether you have any resistance to using sex toys in general, or specifically in your magic. Or whether you're comfortable with the idea of using sex toys in this work, but not certain styles or types. Just notice, and make a note of anything that comes up for you around that with a sense of open curiosity. There is no need for judgement here, but the knowledge you gain may make for some interesting self-exploration. If you do use sex toys, ensure that you keep them clean and in good condition. You can also dedicate them in service of this work, if you choose.

A Reflection

In your foundational magical tool; your magical journal (or Crimson Grimoire), you can reflect on your tools as well. Have a look over the suggestions above and, down one side of your page make note of anything you already have that you'd like to experiment with. Beside these make a note of anything that feels important to you about these items. Are you happy with the pieces you have?

Make a second list below that of things you'd like to use but do not have. Now make notes beside each one of why you feel that it would be worthwhile acquiring, or if you might need to make a substitution. If you cannot burn incense in your space, what would you like to use instead?

Make a third list of things that are not mentioned above but that feel important to you to gather. Beside these items, make a note of why they feel important.

Self-Love Check-In

How are you doing? Has anything excited or unsettled you in this chapter? What might that tell you about yourself? How do you feel about collecting or using magical tools? Or sex toys? The process of gathering materials can be a challenging thought if our budgets are tight, for example, as there can be disappointment around the cost of some of the items on the market which might appeal, but I'm hoping that this chapter has illuminated how inexpensive witchcraft can (and should) be. Considering our physical limitations, due to disabilities or living arrangements for example, can also be challenging. If this is you, I encourage you to draw on your creative power, to explore some of the suggestions for alternatives, and to tune into your most powerful magical tool; your imagination. Your practice will end up much more personal, and powerful, as a result.

Take a few minutes to check in with yourself and make a list of three things, as you have done before.

1. What do you need right now?
2. What do you desire?
3. What are you grateful for?

Go and do at least one thing you need and one thing you desire. Look after yourself and allow yourself to experience pleasure.

Chapter 5

Magical Preparation

The Power of Magic

Magic is real. Whether you consider it to be an external power or the exploration and changing of one's mind, the effects are real, and sometimes unpredictable. It is therefore important to start any working in the right mindset, and with the right energy.

Sexual activity can also have risks, so make sure you have considered the environment you are entering, where and how you intend to perform your practice, and who you might discuss it with. Take the precautions necessary to keep things SSC. If you are using candles, practice fire safety. Ensure your tools are clean. If you are practicing with another then remember to utilize safer sex practices (barrier protection, hygiene, and so on) and consider birth control if you need to. To get yourself and your space right before you start your workings, here are some magical suggestions.

Cleansing

Just as our physical bodies get dirty from the dust of the world, so too can our energetic bodies. Cleansing your physical body keeps the ritual circle and the bedsheets clean. Cleansing your energetic body does the same. Washing with blessed water is a simple way of clearing away energetic muck alongside the physical dust and dirt on your skin. You can bless the water in whatever way makes sense to you, but here is one method of making blessed water. You can make a small amount to wash just your hands and face with, or to mix into a bath of water, or you can make it straight in the bath.

To make a simple blessed water

Hold your hands, palm down, over the salt or herbs you are filling with energy and feel, know, and imagine the bright light of love pouring through you from the universe and into the material until it glows. To strengthen the intention and energy you may say something like:

Creature of earth, may you be filled with love.

Do the same with your water, whether in the basin, the bath, or a vessel, filling it with light and love. You could say:

Creature of water, may you be pure.

Pour the charged salt into the charged water, stirring them together and pouring more love-light into them, saying

Creature of earth and water, may you bring blessings.

You can change the words, and tune into different energies, depending on your intention for the water, but this is a good starting point.

You can use charged soap to support energetic cleansing, just as the blessed water multi-tasks. You may want to choose a soap made with herbs or essential oils known for their cleansing properties (though be wary of allergies). Herbs for cleansing include mugwort, rosemary, sage, and lavender. If you're using essential oils then put a few drops of essential oils into a spoonful or two of base oil such as almond, coconut, or olive first rather than putting it directly into the water. Neat essential oils are very strong and can burn your skin.

Ritual Bath

Run yourself a bath. Light the room with candles to enhance

your experience. Sprinkle blessed water or a palm full of charged salt into the water and visualize it glowing golden. Soak in the bath, wash as normal, and then pull the plug while you are still in the bath watching the water drain away and carry all the dirt away. Rinse yourself off with fresh water or a strained infusion of cleansing herbs.

Ritual Wash

Prepare a basin of warm water with a teaspoon full of charged salt. Wash your face and hands in it. Dip your fingers into the water and sprinkle it over yourself so it feels like rain and washes through your energetic body (aura) around you.

Ritual Shower

Take a shower and visualize the water as golden light washing over you and carrying away energetic crap that needs removing. You can tie a muslin bag of herbs under the shower head, use blessed soap, or rinse with blessed water before, during, or after your shower to include the physical magic.

Shower of Light

If physical cleansing methods are tricky, you can also conjure a cleansing energetic shower. Speak your intention, perhaps with words such as *may I be cleansed and whole*, and visualize a shower of white light that washes over you like a gentle waterfall washing away the murkiness around you. Let the psychic dirt sink into the earth to be composted.

Smoke cleansing

Smoke can have cleansing properties too, for example, burning dried mugwort produces a protective, clearing smoke with lightly psychoactive properties which are said to enhance visions. Again, check for allergies and contraindications before use, as different people will react differently to plants. White sage is traditional in specific cultural contexts, but my experience is that common, garden sage works for me and it grows well in Britain and Europe, without concern over the environment or cultural appropriation. Place a small amount of the herb into a fireproof dish, light with a flame. Hold it at belly height and scoop the smoke up over your body; for example, one scoop washing past your heart and over your head, then one down each side, and then finally one down from your belly to your feet. You may choose to use words such as *By air and fire, may I be purified and strengthened.*

Grounding

As creatures of flesh and spirit, we are beings of the earth and sky combined, moved by both. The mystical bliss of transcendence is tempting, but do not be fooled, there is great power in having your feet on the earth from which you were born.

As creatures of flesh, we can draw on the energy of the physical, and we can anchor ourselves in it. This is grounding. It also, much like the "earth" wire in a plug, earths excess energy and keeps us balanced so we do not fry our circuits when we start raising more power than we are used to. Here are five ways to ground;

~   *Take some time to put your bare feet on the earth outside, hug a tree, and be aware of the land and sky below and above.*

~   *Be aware of your body, moving or resting upon the land. Wiggle your toes, touch your edges, clap your hands. Feel your bones supporting you, and the pressure of the earth supporting you.*

~   *Imagine you are rooted, like a tree, breathing with the earth itself. Be nourished and balanced by the earth of which you are a part.*

~   *Breathe deeply and be aware of your body. Place your hands on the floor and feel any excess energy pouring out in blessing upon the earth, leaving you refreshed and calm.*

~   *Hold a piece of iron, hematite, or a pebble and feel its weight bringing you back down to earth.*

Grounding after magical work is also important to bring you back to the here and now. As well as energetic methods you can re-ground yourself after magic by doing something practical, eating something salty and crunchy, walking barefoot on the earth, putting on the radio or TV, and moving about. Ideally, do something really mundane like vacuum cleaning or sorting the laundry. As a bonus you also get some housework done! Movement, mundanity, and tactile foods all help us to realign our spirits with our bodies if we have performed a pathworking or meditation, and can really help us to integrate what we've gained in magical spaces. I suggest making notes before doing too much, however, to cement your memories.

Alignment

It is not unusual for magical models to use a concept of self as formed of multiple parts – like our spine is formed of multiple vertebrae. One simple way of thinking of this is as energetic, emotional, mental and physical "bodies". These can be out of sync sometimes, the most obvious being when our mind is occupied with a future problem, and our physical body is uncomfortably hunched, forgotten until we try to unfold. When we are present in our bodies, mentally, emotionally, and energetically aligned, we are aware and capable of great things. When our intentions align with our deepest desires, then, too, our magic is more powerful. Simply put, alignment is when all of us is *aligned* towards the same desire.

Listen to your Spirit. Listen to your instincts. Listen to your body, your mind, your heart, your intuition. Notice what the parts of yourself want. Where do they choose the same thing? Where do their desires differ? How can you balance or mediate any conflicts? If your heart needs rest and your body needs to move, what body movement is restful for your heart? Listen and see what you come to understand.

Crafting a Shield

Once we have prepared ourselves it is good to ensure that our energy is contained and that we're not picking up too much energy that isn't ours, as carry around other people's thoughts, emotions, and so on can interfere with our ability to stay grounded or aligned. Sometimes we've built up a layer of psychic dirt as protection from the world and when we clear it away, we feel sensitive, as though there are too many loud noises and bright lights. For our own comfort, to stop ourselves sticking to other people, and to keep ourselves clean as we move through the world, it is worth strengthening our natural energetic skin, often described as "personal shielding".

The following magical practice is designed to take you through the process of coming into alignment, connecting with the earth, clearing and releasing the extra psychic weight you may be carrying, and strengthening those shields. It works with the power of breath and the imagination to bring you home to yourself and it helps build the psychic muscles for future work. If you have been doing this kind of work for a while it is likely that you have encountered similar practices. I invite you to try this variation and see how you find it.

A Magical Practice

The following is a short practice which can be used daily or weekly to strengthen and cleanse oneself. It can also be used to prepare yourself and your space for magic, which I will outline in Chapter 7. Try it as it is laid out for a month and then see what alterations you'd like to make to it.

Breathe in. Be aware of your body.
Breathe out. Release tension and relax.
Breathe in. Be aware of the ground.
Breathe out. Send a root of energy into the earth.
Breathe in. Draw up power from the earth into yourself.
With each breath out, send the root deeper.
With each breath in, draw more power up, filling you.
When you are filled with power and rooted deeply...
Breathe out. Send a cord up into the heavens.
Breathe in. Draw starlight down into you, blending with the earth power.
With each breath out, send the cord higher.
With each breath in, draw more power down.
When you are filled with power and connected strongly...
Breathe out. Let the power that fills you expand out into a sphere.
Breathe in. Pull power up from the earth and down from the stars.
Breathe out. As the sphere expands it pushes the etheric dirt from your self.
Breathe in. Fill with more power.
Breathe out. Let the sphere of power surround you as its edges harden into a shield which allows through only what you choose to allow

~

Breathe with this until it feels clear and strong.
Spend a moment feeling who you are. How is your body? How do you feel? What is important to you? What is in your deepest heart? What is your truest, most divine desire?
Breathe. And let the power you do not need that fills you drain away into the earth and sky. Leaving you in your shield, surrounded by light, protected, clean, and energized. Let the connections fade from mind, but know that your root and your cord to the stars are always there, feeding you.

Consistent Magical Practice

Some useful things to remember for deepening magical and ritual practices include;

~ Engage as many senses as you can to immerse yourself in the magic.

~ Whatever symbols and imagery you use must work for you. Use your sense of aesthetics to tailor your magic to you.

~ Using the same incense, perfume, or scented anointing oil each time will build up a powerful scent-memory that can allow you to conjure the magical state of consciousness and *eros* much faster over time.

~ Make sure you will be uninterrupted so that you are able to concentrate fully on the experience.

~ Use the tools which make you comfortable and support your practice. Background music is a fine addition if it supports your journey, or reminders on your calendar to practice each week.

~ Regular practice builds up magical muscles and helps you to grow more than rare big rituals. Five minutes a day, or half an hour each week, is better than a five hour ritual once a year. But any practice is practice. Do what works for you and allow yourself to enjoy it.

~ Remember that as fun as it is to stay in magical modes of consciousness, it is always better to return fully and earth any excess energy by grounding. If you don't, you may find yourself feeling dizzy, queasy, or scatter-brained.

~ If something works for you, add it to your grimoire so you can find it again later!

~ You may choose to use magical timing in your works, whether you perform your rituals on a Friday (as the day sacred to Venus and the Goddesses of Love and Sex), during a Full Moon (for extra power), at dawn or dusk (as liminal times), at midnight (for the witching hour), at midday (for bringing the sun's beauty and glory into your magic), or simply at the times that you can, is a personal choice. If it seems overwhelming then simply follow your intuition and practice when makes sense to you. Make a note of when you do choose to do your magic and maybe later, you'll notice that you naturally follow a pattern. This may be reflected by the sun, moon, seasons, weather, or something else, or it might reflect your personal cycles.

Self-Love Check-In

How are you doing? How are you feeling after the energetic and magical practices in this chapter? Notice if there is anything you might need to do right now to ground yourself. If any of this was challenging, know that it gets easier with practice. Make a note of where you found things easy, and where you found them hard, and look back on this after you've been working with these regularly for a month or two to remind yourself of how far you'll have come.

Take a few minutes to check in with yourself and, again, make a list of three things:

1.   What do you need right now?
2.   What do you desire?
3.   What are you grateful for?

Go and do at least one thing you need and one thing you desire. Look after yourself and allow yourself to experience pleasure.

Part III
Solo Erotic Magic

Chapter 6

Sex Magic

Forms of Sex Magic

As I have mentioned, sex magic can be broadly classified as having three strands. Magic utilising sex as a method of energy raising, magic for healing sexual issues, or magic to work or unite with the divine as lover.

There are plenty of texts about that discuss the practice of spells fuelled by sexual energy. The simple explanation is that sexual activity raises energy and that energy can be directed towards a goal. Masturbation, for example, can be used to raise personal energy and then sent out to the world through a wish, a visualisation, or focusing on a symbolic representation of the goal desired. The energy can also be poured into a talisman or charm to charge it up and activate the desired effect. Sexual fluids can be used to anoint talismans, magical tools, or the witch themselves, either neat or blended into a base oil. (Do remember to avoid using sexual fluids in places where someone else may come into contact with them without awareness and consent, however, as it is important to do this work safely.) But, if we view our embodied sexuality as shameful, then we cut ourselves off from both pleasure, and this source of personal power.

There are Tantric traditions of avoiding the loss of energy through retaining ejaculate, through orgasming without cumming. There are breathing and muscle exercises to raise power in yourself and build your strength so you can face what may be coming. There are ways of moving energy through your body which will bring pleasure, unblock dis-ease, and encourage release. Historically these practices show that sexual energy has long been understood to be connected to our spiritual health. When it comes to sexual healing there are many folk charms for curing impotence and infertility, but these are not the only kind of sexual issues. If we hold shame around our body or pleasure, if we are divided from our erotic selves, or if we are disconnected from the sexual power that flows through the worlds then we are missing a vital part of our birth right as human beings. This does not mean that one has to desire or engage in sexual activity to be whole and healthy, but rather that we deserve to have access to all of who and what we are, and how the divine erotic manifests in our nature. If we are divine beings, then who are we and what is our divinely erotic nature?

This, then, is where our work must start.

God is Self and Self is God

How would it be to make Goddess come?
What would it take for a smile?
In the mirror She gazed as the power we raised
And Her Love held us safe all the while.

What would life be with a lover divine?
What if Her blessings rained down?
A gift from the gods, oh now what were the odds
That my offering would be deemed fine?

Now my wishes were granted and my cup overflowed,
I could tell it was Her that I'd seen.
How could I know, before that afterglow
That an invitation was all that She needs?

Wholly Divinely Erotic

In this way, sex magic is love magic; not the enchantment of another, but the seduction of oneself.

The path to sexual healing is a long one, one might even say the work of a lifetime, but that doesn't mean that we can't make a start. Every day gives us a chance to learn to fall back in love with ourselves, to remember and reclaim our power over our own pleasure. Each of us will have very different journeys to take, and different chains to break or wounds to heal, and so one of the most important things in choosing to engage with this path is to trust our own sense of timing and rightness, and to get support when we need it.

Be gentle with yourself, and be proud of taking things at your own pace. That, in itself, is an act of self-love and acceptance.

I invite you to begin a courtship with yourself. To look at this aspect of your Craft as a gentle, loving, seduction of your divine being. Approach this journey as an opportunity to court your own sense of pleasure, as an offering and devotion to the part of you that is divine.

Each of the pieces of magic below can be done as exercises, but I invite you to treat them as something sacred, as ritual workings in and of themselves. Set aside some time, like you would for a date with a loved one. You may want to set aside time on a Friday, ruled by the planet Venus, and sacred to Freya, Aphrodite, and the goddesses of love and passion. Use any magic you already practice to support this work. This is for you, so make it yours. I recommend that you begin each working with the magical practice from Chapter 5 and the invocation from Chapter 2. You can find a version of both put together in a ritual outline in the appendices which weaves together pieces from later in this book as well.

Dressing for a Date

Prepare yourself for magic, in whatever way feels right for you. Think of the time ahead as being an important date with your beloved and allow yourself to feel the excitement that comes from anticipation. You may like to choose your clothing accordingly, and dress for the occasion. Perhaps there is a perfume or scent you feel particularly confident or sexy in. Allow the thought of being your own beloved, your own lover, to wrap itself around you and inspire your preparations. It might feel silly at first, but see if you can allow yourself that childlike innocence in the game of "yes, but what if...". What if you were dressing for your beloved, and your beloved was you?

If you would like some suggestions, perhaps take a magical bath with blessed water and rose petals for love. You may want to choose some music which feels loving or sexy to you, I personally like having instrumental music playing for most solo magical work I do. Take a few moments to centre yourself and breathe slowly and calmly. Take seven deep breaths, in and out. Place one hand on your belly and one on your heart and just be present with yourself for a moment. Set your intention that this time is for your own healing and pleasure, and is a time for you to be with yourself in love, to whatever degree that works for you right now.

After your magic-dates, make sure you take a few moments to connect to the earth beneath you, and imagine yourself wrapped in a blanket of love by the Divinity of the Universe. Make note of anything you'd like to remember, as magical experiences are like dreams and will often slip from your mind, and have something to eat to let any energy you have shifted or raised settle.

An Altar to Love

If we want to work with something in our lives,
then we must make space for that work.

Choose a surface to create an altar to *eros;* the Divine Erotic, Divine Love, Divine Pleasure. Before you begin, gather together whatever you might like to include as visual representations of these qualities. What scents might conjure love and pleasure for you? What textures and sensual objects might you include? Are there sounds that you might like to include, like a windchime, or a music box? What elements feel like they might fit? Perhaps a jug of water for flow and nourishment, or a dish of soil for being embodied, or a red candle for passion? Choose a couple of items, and perhaps a coloured or textured cloth to cover the surface before you begin. Play with your senses, and feed those that work for you.

If you do not have a surface to work with, perhaps you have a box or a bag that you can place a cloth and some objects in. When you want to invoke these energies in your space, open the container, lay out the cloth, and place the objects in a pattern that feels right in the moment. See what stories they tell by their relationships.

If none of these things speak to you, you may decide to create a picture instead, to hang on the wall, or keep inside the cover of your journal if you need to be discreet. An image which you can add to over time as your relationship with this magic and your divine self deepens and grows. Or even a song, poem, or story, if you are that way inclined.

In this way we explore the imagery of love and pleasure, and the energies of the divine erotic in a gentle way. By making an altar or shrine or dedicated container we build a guest house for it in our lives, which perhaps may become a permanent room, to remind ourselves of the importance of this work to us, and to invite those energies to dance with us.

Spend time with your altar, clean it regularly, handle the objects, meditate on what they mean to you. Each Friday, full moon, festival, or other regular time period, take a moment to ask yourself what needs to change on your altar, and notice what that tells you about the dance between you and this magic.

Tuning into Pleasure as Magic

Life is magic moving bones made of stardust

Bring something sensual, that you find pleasure in, into your magical space. It might be dancing, self-massage, painting. It might be a delicious treat that delights or brings sweet comfort when eaten. It might be singing, relaxing to music, playing a drum, lighting a candle, or even rebuilding your altar.

Bring yourself into your magical space and begin to engage with the thing you enjoy and, as you do, notice the pleasure it brings you. Notice, not just the enjoyment or the thing itself, but the way it feels in your body, the way your own magic begins to rise as your delight does. Notice that you begin to glow with the bliss of doing something you love.

Notice how, in your body, this is very similar to safe, healthy, erotic pleasure. You may feel more alive, more relaxed, more energised. This is lifeforce flowing through you. This is the divine erotic, the pleasure of the body, as magic. Not restricted to sexual acts, but rooted deeply in our existence as embodied beings drawn to, empowered, and healed by embodied pleasure.

Return to this as often as you like, to take the time to remember how that embodied pleasure, that erotic aspect of yourself, is safe and beautiful and divine.

Notice when you feel this way outside of the magical space, too. Notice when the pleasure of walking through the forest, or breathing in a fresh breeze, or wearing something soft and sensual, feels like magic. And when you notice, breathe it in and let yourself sigh with happiness at how wonderful life can be.

Self-Loving

You are your best lover.

Make sure you have plenty of time when you will be undisturbed so you can relax and enter your magical space with whichever toys or items you enjoy using for self-pleasure. Take your time finding your centre and use your mirror or other senses to recognise and greet yourself as your beloved. Undress yourself and take time to really enjoy the process, remembering to treat yourself as your own beloved, a willing lover who you are gently seducing. Speak to yourself, out loud or in your thoughts, as you would a lover. Touch yourself in ways that feel good. Explore yourself with love. And take time to make love to yourself, in whatever way, and to whatever extent, is right for you right now. As you do, allow yourself to feel the pleasure as magic and, if you choose to orgasm, release that magic as a blessing which rains back down upon you and the earth beneath you.

Return to this as often as you like, and begin to notice the energy that pleasure raises as it moves through your body. Remember to breathe, and notice how your breath supports and directs that movement of energy. Let it wash through you and gently dissolve any blockages that it encounters that you feel ready to release.

Notice how you feel afterward. Be kind to yourself. After this piece of magic especially, remember to come back to your everyday self gently to allow time for the experience to integrate with your everyday way of being.

Drinking Stars

Whispered prayer over water,
Love letter to the gods.
Unbound
I drink in their power
and a galaxy swirls within me.
Red dwarves in my belly,
Golden suns in fingertips,
Dark earth below my toes
waiting while I descend again, a meteor aglow
With all the glory of the stars.

We are stardust, they say,
I disagree.
In the pure, velvet night,
we are starlight.

Self-Love Check-In

How are you doing? Has anything excited or unsettled you in this chapter? What might that tell you about yourself? Remember that it is important to work through these pieces at the pace that suits you. There is no rush. You have had your whole life to get to the point you are at now, that which you have already gained took time, and you have plenty of time to deepen, heal, and grow now.

Take a few minutes to check in with yourself and make a list of three things, as we have done in each chapter.

1. What do you need right now?
2. What do you desire?
3. What are you grateful for?

Go and do at least one thing you need and one thing you desire. Look after yourself and allow yourself to experience pleasure.

Chapter 7

Glamourie

Charmed, I'm sure

Once, *Glamourie* meant an enchantment or illusion. Over time it came to be associated with beauty, specifically the kind of beauty that models and Hollywood stars are expected to have, reminding us of its roots in the concept of illusion; the glamour of the camera, conveyed through make-up and the performance of sexiness. It is also, however, used to describe someone who holds that kind of charm naturally. One who presents themselves as hauntingly beautiful, who moves with grace and charm, may be said to be *glamorous*.

In this chapter then, when I use the term glamourie, I am weaving the concept of beauty and magic together, not as illusion, but as illumination. Each of us has a beauty in the magic within, in the light that we carry and in the sensual confidence of embodiment. Media has long worked to convince us that beauty is hard to acquire, that it costs money and takes effort. The nature of the world, and of ourselves as creatures of this earth, suggests that that is only the case if we are seeking a specific form of artificial beauty. The expression of this beauty, of our sensual selves moving with love through the world, is a glamour. It is a shining of magic and a sharing of pleasure through expression and creativity, confidence and presence.

Still, it can be hard to find confidence in that natural expression when we're used to hiding ourselves, and even more so when we have yet to recognise the beauty that we hold within. Now, then, we seek to view ourselves with love and to find our own inner power of *glamourie*.

A Reflection

In your journal, pause to reflect for a moment.

How do you express eros *already in your life?*
How comfortable are you in your own sensual beauty?
How comfortable are you in expressing your full self as a sexual being?
What clothes, colours, and situations make you feel safest and most like you are fully your erotic self?

The Performance of Glamourie in the World

When exploring *glamourie*, the expression of our erotic selves, it is important to remain aware of our boundaries, as well as the boundaries of where and how we are expressing our selves. There are some people who assume that an expression of sexuality is an invitation, or an expression of desire, but that is not true. We may choose to dress up for another, but we may also choose to dress up for ourselves. In the same way we may choose to express our sensual, embodied, erotic nature to communicate desire to a particular person, or we may choose to express *eros* because we are rooting into our wholeness and learning to live more authentically and fully in the world. Sexual expression is not the same as sexual desire or attraction, and one can be a highly sexual being whilst having no interest in *having sex* with anyone, whether in that moment or ever.

To put it bluntly, sex is important to me, but that does not mean it is something I share with everybody. It is precious, and I get to choose where and when I am open to connecting with someone sexually. As do you. Arousal is not an invitation. The erotic is not sexual activity.

It can be important, then, to choose when and where we express our erotic selves in our preferred ways in order to protect our boundaries, and to move safely through the world. And many of us know this already, which is often the reason we have buried this expression entirely, or over-perform it in defiance.

A Reflection

Take up your journal and ask yourself, gently, about your boundaries.

In what ways do you hide where you don't need to?
In what ways do you perform sexiness, rather than expressing your divine erotic self?
Where are your boundaries around attention? What are you comfortable with? What are you not comfortable with?
In the place that you live, where can you express that part of yourself safely?
How do you feel about the idea that you don't owe anyone an expression of eros? That you don't owe anyone modesty? That you don't owe anyone anything sexual at all, for any reason?
What are the stories you carry around the expression of erotic power which are holding you back from feeling fully alive and in your power?

Read over the following ritual and consider whether there are stories that others told you about being sexual that you have internalised and that block you from being fully alive. These old lies which we pick up and carry with us are like chains that we choose to keep hold of. They may be comforting, and they may have been given to us in a misguided attempt to keep us safe. They may even have kept us safe, once upon a time, but if they now hold us back from living fully, from stepping into our embodied, sensual power, then we can choose to discard them. Or, as they are made of energy, of our energy, we can choose to transform the chains into a blessing to support us in moving forward.

A Ritual; The Pyre of Old Lies

Find a fireproof dish, and ensure it is on a fireproof surface. If you need to, you can set this up outside, and do the ritual in two parts. Safety first.

Open your sacred space and, on a fresh piece of paper, spend some time writing down the old stories that keep you from trusting in your own beauty. Write down the lies that people have told you about yourself. Write down the words and thoughts that play within your mind when you consider your own self-expression.

Once you have as many on the page as you can bring yourself to write today.

Feel yourself pouring the old blocks that those words had become in your body into the paper.

Fold it up into a triangle, with the old words inside, like a curse to be broken.

Write on the outside the old formula of disappearing;

ABRACADABRA
BRACADABR
RACADAB
ACADA
CAD
A

Then, take it to your fireproof dish and set it on fire, and feel yourself warmed by the flames as the old curse is transformed into brightness to feed your soul. Gather the ashes and take them back to your altar. Mix a little bit of the ash with a little water or ink. Take a new piece of paper and write yourself a blessing with the ashes. Do something that makes you feel loved. Close your sacred space.

Ground yourself afterward and place your blessing in your grimoire or on your altar where you will see it, where it can support you in your next steps.

Finding Our own Beauty

How we present to the world is how we interface with it. We offer up some part of ourselves to every person we meet and we know ourselves in part through how we are mirrored back to ourselves. And how we feel about ourselves effects our self-confidence and, thus, our power, our lifeforce.

If beauty is something you value, consider whether casting a glamour of beauty is something that might be important to you. If power, then ponder how to express power. But, more than that, consider how to allow the core you that you are to shine through. Not the warped, funhouse mirror of false humility, wherein we tear ourselves down and keep ourselves smaller than we are... but rather the true, brilliant, shimmering core of truth and magic that animates and haunts the stardust of our flesh.

If the only mirror you carry of yourself is crafted of insults, failure, and rejection, that doesn't mean that is all that you are, it only means that those are the things we have been encouraged to craft our mirror from. Glamour magic begins with breaking that mirror and rebuilding it to show the shining, gorgeous, essence of yourself.

Take up your journal and ask yourself;

How do I choose to express my eros, my lifeforce?
What is important to me about how I express myself?
How is it important to me to be seen? Why might that be?
What is the starlight that I carry?

Mirror work

The simplest thing, and the hardest thing, can be to see yourself. Sit at your altar or clear a space and place a candle and a mirror on a safe surface in front of you. Dim any room lights and light the candle with the intention of looking at yourself as you would look at someone you love. Gaze into your eyes in the mirror and just be with yourself for a few minutes.

Once this feels reasonably comfortable, you can take this one step further and smile at yourself, allow yourself to feel kindly towards the person in the mirror. Notice their beauty and let your recognition of their goodness be reflected back at them through your smile. Allow yourself to receive their smile in return.

You can also practice listening to your voice as you speak, sing, or hum. Try telling yourself how lovely they are, how much you love them, how gorgeous their voice is. Use something to record and play back your voice and see how that feels. Listen as though you are listening to someone else, someone you care about. Notice the best in your own voice, as you would with your own beloved.

Explore the other senses too, if you are comfortable; stroke your arms, legs, sides. Touch or massage your hands, feet, thighs, belly. Notice how lovely you feel. Smell your own skin, with and without any scents you choose to wear, and explore how that is for you. Some aromatherapists will sniff their inner elbow to 'reset' their noses in between the strong essential oil smells. Your skin may have a different scent when you've been out in the sun, or fresh from the shower, or if you have eaten certain spices. Can you notice these things without ascribing a sense of right or wrong, good or bad to them? Can you explore them as sensations which, perhaps, might be enjoyable and pleasurable? Can you take the step to finding the loveliness of these parts of your physical life?

Perhaps choose a different sense each time and gently learn to recognise in yourself what you would recognise in a beloved one, and thus what they might recognise in you.

The Magic of Self-Portraits

Sometimes it can be hard to see the beauty and sensuality of yourself. We learn to see our flaws early on and, just like when we look at a piece of our own art, or taste a meal we've cooked, or observe anything which we have made, we see where we, or our those created pieces of our souls, do not match up to the idealised vision we have of what could be. We hold ourselves to impossible standards and so we fall short.

And yet, others can see the value of us. Our beauty. Our vibrancy. Our loveliness. Our friends and lovers will often highlight the best bits of ourselves to us, because that is what they see. And don't we do the same to them? What if we could do that for ourselves?

This is part of the value of self-portraits, through them we can start to show ourselves the things about ourselves which we find beautiful. Make of it a ritual, a spellcasting for the confidence of glamour. For what is glamour but the projection of that which is awesome in yourself?

If you are a visual creature, take your camera in hand and turn it to yourself. Ask yourself what you would see if you were looking at the person viewed through the camera lens as someone you cared for. Spend some time highlighting those parts of your physical self which you enjoy.

If you desire; add make-up, pull out your favourite clothes, apply filters. Pick angles that make you feel good. Show yourself what you love about yourself.

Sink into the other senses. Explore listening to your voice, speaking in different tones, singing, humming, whispering your favourite poetry or prayers. Record short pieces and listen back as though it were your beloved. Explore the sensation of fabrics, of flowing skirts that swish as you move, of velvets or silken shirts. What feels good to wear. Explore the sounds of tiny bells on jewellery or woven into your hair. Of wooden beads that click together as you move. Listen to the sound of the fabrics sliding against each other. Explore different perfumes or shampoos. What smells amazing on your skin, your hair? Play... seek pleasure in all things and notice when the stories you were told over the years disrupt the enjoyment you are finding. Let them go. Tell yourself a new story because the old stories, they often lie.

A little illustration: As a child I wore yellow as often as I could. I loved it. The brightness and joy in it delighted me. Then, one day, someone told me it was the colour of jaundice, and that it made me look ill. Overnight I disavowed yellow. I refused to wear it for decades, right up until one summer, not that long ago... There was a carnival coming, an event made for playfulness. There were a pair of bright yellow boots in a second-hand shop, and a supportive partner. A bee costume emerged and, through it, I found my wings. Oh, and that yellow looked damn good on me. I've got the pictures to prove it.

Make a record of how these things make you feel, when you feel like your shining, magical, self is being embodied in how you are presenting yourself, then make sure you have something physical to remind you of this feeling later. Choose an outfit that incorporates some of what you've learned, print that selfie and put it somewhere you'll see it often, wear that wonderful scent or carry a handkerchief with a few drops of it on with you. Or, maybe, write it down. Whatever will help you remember how stunning you are when you're seen by someone who says "those old stories are lies that hold no power over me."

Blessed Jewellery

Talismans are wonderful tools; they help us carry the magic we have spun in our rituals out into our daily lives. A specially chosen piece of jewellery, blessed with the magic of self-love, can be such a talisman. If you enjoy wearing jewellery, choose a piece that you feel holds the message of the Divine Erotic for you and, before you bless it, cleanse it. If it is safe to immerse in water or smoke you may choose to bathe it as you would your body, as in Part II. If not, use the light visualisation, or your favourite way of cleansing objects.

During your ritual time, spend some time at your altar, exploring pleasure, taking glamour-selfies, listening to beauty, and bathing in Divine Pleasure. Let the magic rise. You can raise power using physical self-pleasuring techniques too, if you so desire.

Hold your talisman to your heart and Will it to be infused by the magic that surrounds you and fills you. Let it reflect the light of your candle and see it glow with power. Energy flows where you focus, so you can pour all that goodness into your talismanic object, until it hums and radiates with pleasure and love. Say some words that feel like a sealing of the magic to you, perhaps; *So mote it be* or *As I Will, so it is done.* Now put it on. Feel the magic it holds. Feel how it carries that blessing for you.

Each day that you wear it, whenever you feel need of it, touch it and remember the magic you carry. Remember the pleasure it carries. Let it bathe you and bless you in that magic again.

If you ever feel like it starts to lose its charm, then cleanse and bless it again. In later blessings you can experiment with a shorter ritual, or a prayer to one of the Powers of Pleasure, such as a deity, who we will meet together soon.

Self-Blessing Ritual to Reclaim our Power

In naming ourselves beautiful, handsome, gorgeous, sexy, divine, we reclaim our power from the world. We choose how we will see ourselves, how we will express ourselves. From here we can begin to recognise, not just intellectually but in our bodies, that we hold the power to change the judgements we have made about ourselves.

As witches, we do this through magic, through ritual. This is one thing a self-blessing ritual can be used for.

In this ritual, then, you choose to reclaim your own expression by blessing yourself, and naming yourself as divine, recognising that you are an embodiment of the Divine power of the Universe, spirit expressed and manifested as the physical.

Find a time when you can be undisturbed for at least an hour. Acquire an oil that you can safely put on your skin, plain olive oil or coconut oil will work, or a massage oil such as almond or grapeseed. You can even use baby oil, or, if oil is not available or suitable, water will do. If you can get dried rose petals, or other dried flowers, then you may choose to make an infused blessing oil (or water infusion), using the recipes at the end of this ritual.

A Pre-Ritual Reflection

You may choose to journal on your favourite things about yourself.

- ~ What makes you feel confident, sexy, powerful, or beautiful?
- ~ If you could, how would you choose to feel from now on?
- ~ And finally, and most importantly, what does, or would, being your own beloved feel like?

Preparation

- ~ Choose a fresh candle in white, or an appropriate colour.
- ~ Gather your blessing oil.
- ~ Make yourself a drink that you find pleasurable.
- ~ Have a bath, shower, or wash with the intention of washing away any negative images you have of yourself.

The Ritual

Place your candle on your altar, unlit for now. Perform the Foundational Magical Practice from Chapter 5, expanding the power into a sacred circle;

Breathe in. Be aware of your body.
Breathe out. Release tension and relax.
Breathe in. Be aware of the ground.
Breathe out. Send a root of energy into the earth.
Breathe in. Draw up power from the earth into yourself.

With each breath out, send the root deeper.
With each breath in, draw more power up, filling you.
When you are filled with power and rooted deeply...
Breathe out. Send a cord up into the heavens.
Breathe in. Draw starlight down into you, blending with the
earth power.
With each breath out, send the cord higher.
With each breath in, draw more power down.
When you are filled with power and connected strongly...
Breathe out. Let the power that fills you expand out into a sphere.
Breathe in. Pull power up from the earth and down from the stars.
Breathe out. As the sphere expands it pushes the etheric dirt from
your self.
Breathe in. Fill with more power.
Breathe out. Let the sphere of power surround you and expand out
into a sphere of protective golden light that surrounds you and
your space, the edges becoming a sacred circle to safely hold you.

Light your candle with an invocation to the Divine Lover;

A breath of bliss, caught upon the tongue,
I welcome you, invite you; Divine Lover, come.
Red Goddess dancing, spinning like the sun,
Wild God and Bright Spirit; come, lovers, come.
Bless my heart, my mind, my skin,
with touch of pleasure welcomed in,
in your honour I begin,
Divine Lover, come!

And rest awhile in their presence, in the energy of Love and *eros*.
Let the energy wash over you, fill you, and bathe you in love,
healing and wholeness.

When you are ready, take up the oil and dip your fingers into it.

~ Anoint your forehead in blessing saying; *I am Divine, whole and complete in myself.*

~ Anoint your throat in blessing saying; *I express my self, my truth, my love.*

~ Anoint your heart in blessing saying; *I am loved by the universe, and beloved of myself.*

~ Anoint your belly in blessing saying; *I hold the power to transform all that I take in.*

~ Anoint your genitals in blessing saying; *I am deserving of pleasure.*

~ Anoint your feet in blessing saying; *I am a child of this earth, whole and complete in myself.*

Feel the energy of *eros* around and within you, your sexual power as part of the lifeforce of the Divine. Feel yourself, named as Divine child of the Earth. And feel the strength and beauty of yourself in this moment.

Raise your drink in a toast to yourself and to *eros*, and say a blessing upon yourself and your divine erotic power;

I am Divine and I bless myself.
I am of the earth and I shape myself.
I am Beloved, and Beloved of myself.
I am eros incarnate.

Spend as long as you like in this space, with this energy. You may choose to simply be present, or you may choose to make love to yourself, as your own beloved. When you are ready, thank the divine erotic;

Lovers three I honour you,
Let your blessings flow,
Know that you are welcome here,
and help my magic grow.

Let me know your sacred ways,
Of love and sex divine,
For now I bid you kind farewell,
You to your homes and me to mine.

Breathe into your core for a moment and centre yourself in your body. As you breathe, let the excess power that fills you, any which you do not need, drain away into the earth and sky. Let the sphere of light shrink around you, until you are in your shield, surrounded by light, protected, clean, and energized. Let the connections to earth, sky, and *eros* fade from mind, but know that your root and your cord to the stars are always there, feeding you.

Make any notes in your journal that you feel you would like to remember. Finally, go and do something mundane and grounding, bringing yourself back to everyday consciousness before jumping into the rush of the world if you can.

You may wish to keep the oil on your altar and to anoint yourself each morning, repeating the self-blessing, to bring that energy and power more deeply into yourself and your life. Notice how this makes you feel over time.

Love Blessing Oil

Two small, clean jars, or a jar and a bottle
Dried rose petals (or other body safe flowers of your choosing)
Enough oil to fill the jar
A sieve or strainer

1. Loosely fill one jar with petals.
2. Cover the petals with oil saying a prayer such as;

Divine Spirit bless this oil
Let its touch be filled with love

3. Place the oil upon your altar for a month.
4. Shake it gently each day, repeating the prayer as you do.
5. Strain the oil in to the second jar (or bottle) and label it with the date and contents. You might write the prayer you have used on the label too, so that it continues to add its blessing to the oil, and so that you can find it again easily when using the oil.

   Note: Ensure the flowers are completely dry to prevent them becoming mouldy in the oil.

Love Blessing Infusion (if oil is unsuitable)

A palmful of rose flower petals
A clean jar or cup
A sieve or strainer

1. Hold the petals in your palms and pour love into them.
2. Place them in the jar.
3. Pour freshly boiled water over the petals saying the prayer above, or one similar.
4. Allow the magic and scent to infuse the water for five minutes, or until the water has cooled.
5. Strain out the petals if you choose.
6. Ensure the water is cool enough to touch comfortably before use.

Dates with The Divine Erotic

Do you read erotica? Do you engage with art that contains the kiss of *eros*? When we engage with ethical erotic art which others have created, we meet their expression of sacred pleasure with the rising *eros* in ourselves. We can explore the erotic energy that flows through us by engaging with fantasies and stories, and, if it is in our nature, by expressing beauty and embodied pleasure ourselves. This may come in the form of sensual dancing, spoken word performance, offering our lover sensual touch, or in other ways. We may express our pleasure at being alive entirely within a private space, for our eyes only, or we may share expressions through videos, writing, photography, painting, song, and more, in (appropriate) public spaces. The sharing of erotic art is an important part of allowing *eros* to flow in sacred and safe ways within culture. As we know, repression is unhealthy, and so finding ways to share that honour your own boundaries and those of others are important. And there are plenty of spaces to do that within.

We often encounter these kinds of creations with judgment, or reservation, because we are uncomfortable with our own sexual nature. Or, alternatively, with a degree of desensitisation. I offer the ritual below as a way to engage with the sacred nature of the *eros* behind the erotica.

A Ritual; Sharing in Sacred Erotica

Read the below ritual components and choose which option you would like to do. Or, use them as inspiration to engage with a different kind of material, or to engage in a somewhat different way which works for you.

Gather together poetry, prose, music, and art which inspires that sense of vibrant aliveness which is the hallmark of *eros*, that erotic charge of being turned-on and delighted, and give yourself space to indulge in the enjoyment of it, and begin courting *eros*. Perform the opening, then your choice of engagement, then the closing.

Opening the Ritual

Prepare your space and clear some time, and bring whatever you need to enjoy your chosen creative expressions of the erotic. You may choose to do this in the bedroom, in the bath, at your altar, or in whichever space feels most decadent to you.

Light a candle and incense, or set the mood with lighting

and scent as suits you. Make yourself a drink that you find delicious and sensual, whether that is wine, hot chocolate, a latte, sparkling cordial, a smoothie, or something else. It may even be a simple glass of cool water with ice cubes and a slice of lemon. Pour a second drink as an offering for *eros* and the divine erotic powers and place that somewhere that makes sense, perhaps on your altar.

Perform the foundational magical practice in Chapter 5 and continue breathing into the sphere, extending your energetic circle out to contain the whole space as a magical circle.

Drink your chosen drink while contemplating *eros* and the divine erotic within you and within the world.

Choose one of the following suggestions for enjoying your chosen material, and enjoy.

Option 1; Reading erotic poetry
In your sacred space choose a selection of poetry. Read them slowly, out loud, feeling the shape and power of the words, the rhythm of them, the taste of them on your tongue. Feel how your body and mind respond. Read them like invocations, or like love letters to *eros*.

Allow yourself time between each one to feel the magic of *eros* surround you and move through you. Luxuriate.

Option 2; Listening to erotic music
In your sacred space, put a playlist or album of erotic music on. Get comfortable and rest in the music, let it surround your body. Feel it in your muscles and bones. Feel the music flowing through you, caressing you with pleasure. Allow *eros* to touch you through the music.

Option 3; Worshiping eros through images
Make yourself comfortable and gaze upon the visual art you've chosen. Treat these as sacred icons of the divine erotic power in

the world. Set them up on your altar and direct your attention to them as focal points for worshiping the power they represent. Notice in your body and spirit the feeling that resonates in you, reflected in these expressions of *eros* which called to you, which showed you a part of that magic in yourself and the world. Allow yourself to express reverence and worship of the magic of *eros* through these images, and allow *eros* to be invoked in you through them in return.

Option 4; Creating Erotic Media as Self Expression

Spend some time contemplating *eros*. Breathe into the feeling of sacred sexual and divine erotic power within yourself. Feel it in your body and spirit. Allow images, words, movements, sensations, and responses to arise in you. Take up your tools and begin to create from this sensation.

~   If you dance, then dance.
~   If you write, then write.
~   If you paint, then paint.
~   If you sing, then sing.
~   If you sculpt, then sculpt.
~   If you model, then model.

Allow yourself to express this magic through your creative skills. You may choose to record your dancing, song, spoken words, modelling, or other creative expression, or you may keep it in the moment.

Allow a few days after the event for the energies to settle, and then you may choose to share your creation in a space suitable for such sharing, or you may keep it private. In this, honour your boundaries and comfort levels, and respect both yourself and others. If what you create is explicit, ensure that you share it only in spaces where that is appropriate, and only in ways that are sensible for you. Allowing a few days before sharing can help to make these choices with a clear head.

Option 5; Courting The Divine Erotic

Perhaps none of the above options quite work for you, in that case, use them as inspiration or a basic recipe to adapt to something that does. You may find that you listen best to music by dancing to it. In which case, dance. Maybe your choice of erotic expression is in make up or costuming, in which case perhaps you gather your inspiration and, in sacred space, paint your face and body, or costume yourself, in response to the flow of *eros*. Perhaps you find *eros* in the feel of your fingers in rich, dark, moist, soil, and designing your next flowerbed is the most divinely erotic experience that you want to court *eros* with. And perhaps you find *eros* in the cinema, and you share a toast in ritual space beforehand, dress up nicely and take yourself and *eros* out for a date to the cinema, returning to your space afterward to record the experience and express gratitude. You know yourself best. Gather your materials and create the perfect date. Just remember not to leave the candles burning if you are elsewhere.

Closing the Ritual

When it is time to close up, spend a moment in gratitude for that which you have experienced, and begin to pay attention to your breathing again. Release any energy that has built up which you do not need, sending it on an outbreath to bless your life with more pleasure and beauty. And allow your magic circle to contract, like a mist shrinking down to a sphere that just sits around you comfortably, remembering your connection to the earth, and your nature as embodied in the here and now.

Take a moment to breathe into your centre and let the experience you have just had settle into your bones and warm your heart. Make any notes you'd like to remember in your grimoire.

Extinguish the candle and incense still burning, and leave the space to do something grounding and mundane.

Dispose of the offering to *eros* in whatever way is practical.

Self-Love Check-In

How are you feeling? Has anything excited or unsettled you in this chapter? What might that tell you about yourself? This chapter can be either really easy, or really difficult for people, depending on your relationship with yourself. Approach each piece playfully, gently, and with kindness for yourself. You can return to these exercises and thoughts as often as you like or need.

Take a few minutes to check in with yourself and make a list of three things, as we did in the previous chapters.

1. What do you need right now?
2. What do you desire?
3. What are you grateful for?

Go and do at least one thing you need and one thing you desire. Remember that you are deserving of love and pleasure.

Chapter 8

The Foundations of Sexual Spellcasting

Sex and Power

If you ever tell someone you do "sex magic", this is probably what they think of, so I'd be remiss to leave it out.

Sexual activity can raise a lot of power. It tends to involve rhythmic physical exertion, which is a time honoured method of reaching a non-everyday state-of-mind and generating energy for magic, through activities such as drumming, dancing, spinning, and rocking. It is also an activity which is literally related to creating life, which is something that takes at least a certain amount of energy too.

In terms of sympathetic magic, for example then, one can fertilise an idea, to then incubate over time and birth it when it is ready, or use that burst of energy as the raw material to fuel the manifestation itself. In either instance the process is relatively straightforward, though keeping your attention on the goal at the appropriate moment may take practice.

The most ethical option for this process is masturbation as then you are free to concentrate on your desire without involving another person, or inviting them to join you in a sacred activity only to have your attention be elsewhere. If, however, you have a sexual and magical partner who is keen on making magic with you, then you can both choose your goals together, and direct the energy together. If this is a new process to you, however, it is best to start solo.

Sexual Spellcasting

Firstly, set your goal. Whether that is a seed that you'll nurture to completion in the future, or something that needs a final push to manifest right now is your choice. You may decide on a mantra, sigil, talisman, or similar to represent it. Ensure that is prepared beforehand and that any mantra is well memorised. Remember to keep your goal in line with your ethics, and consider any questions of consent or potential unintended outcomes carefully.

Next, clear your space and prepare yourself. Cleansing to clear away any mental or energetic distractions not related to the goal is important, otherwise you can pour the energy you raise into those instead.

Then, begin your sexual activity, feeling the energy building within you. Keep your goal in mind as clearly as you can throughout. When you are ready, allow yourself to release that energy, directing it to manifest your goal through intention, imagination, and mantra or other focal point. Do your best to stay focused on your goal, but don't stress about it if you get distracted.

The longer you can hold off on orgasm, the more energy you are likely to raise. Orgasm isn't necessary for the release, either, send the energy toward your goal in the way that suits you. A sharp out breath or sound might be suitable, for example, as long as you're releasing and directing the energy. If you are multi-orgasmic, then you can build the power with each orgasm and have each one be a reinforcement, adding more strength to the spell each time.

That, honestly, is the core of sexual spellcasting. Simple, though not necessarily easy as it requires self-control and mental focus during a point when letting go of control is built in.

If you are not squeamish, and do not have any STIs for example, you may also choose to gather the sexual fluids produced during this process and use it to bless your personal tools, or self. Obviously in these instances it is important to practice safer sex protocols and to avoid applying these fluids to anything anyone else might come into contact with. It is also not a good idea to keep these fluids as they do not contain preservatives. If you are squeamish, however, then this particular avenue of magic is probably not for you!

Once you have practiced raising energy through masturbation, and concentrating on your goal while you release and direct that energy, and you and your partner have decided to engage in this practice together, then the key is to both be very clear about exactly what the purpose of the magic is, and to be in alignment with your vision and goals. Ensure that both parties are consenting to both the activity and the magic, freely and without coercion, as partners.

The very act of facing the taboo of sex and magic, of spirit in the sticky, messy, physicality of sexual activity, can be a powerful way of boosting your magic and spiritual life in and of itself. In engaging with it we find that the culturally shameful act of pleasure is inherently something which aligns body and soul and can heal the division forced upon us between being "good" and being embodied.

"I eat fear for breakfast"

Do not fear the lion that lives within your bones,
Prowling through your sinews as you pivot on your toes.
Do not fear the roar that rises joyful from your core
As you feel the pulse of life so pure fear not to declare "more"!
Embrace the gorgeous glory of the sun upon your mane
as you bask in beauty wild and vast out upon the plains.
Let the starlight guide you as your paws pad concrete streets
Because even in the darkness you will find a tender feast.
Do not fear the lion that lives within your bones
Prowling growling glory from your crown down to your toes.

The Ritual Challenge

How do you enter this circle?
In perfect love and perfect trust.

When we step into the circle of magic it is not unusual to be challenged at the entrance, to be met by a blade and a question that requires a declaration and a commitment before you may enter. In some traditions this is formalised, but in other paths it can vary from ritual to ritual, and in magical practice as a whole, the challenge is there at every step of the way. To walk a magical path, we must set aside our reservations and sense of propriety, our concerns at being judged, and to immerse ourselves with trust in the magic and the spirits we work with. To walk the path is to face the challenge;

How do you take this path?

Every step is an answer to the question.

In love and trust, come what may.

It is a declaration that we will strive to enact our magic in this way; trusting in the magic, offering love, wholly and deeply committed to that which we are doing.

When one adds sex into the mix, an important aspect of our human existence which is viewed with some distrust, there is an extra layer of challenge. Can we commit to healing the damage we have sustained in our lives around sex and spirit? Can we trust that we are doing right when we may appear to be going against what we were taught about being good and pure? Can we hold sexual pleasure and spirituality together in our hearts with love?

How do you walk the path of the divine erotic magic within?

We bring all of ourselves to the answer, our love and our wounds, our hope and our fears, our flesh and our spirit, because only when we do can we find the way to wholeness.

With all my heart.

Self-Love Check-In

How are you feeling? Has anything excited or unsettled you in this chapter? What might that tell you about yourself? In some ways this is the easiest magic of all contained in these chapters. Identifying your desire, raising power, and letting go. In other ways, it might bring up some doubts for you around whether you deserve what you desire, whether magic really can bring you anything, whether you are capable of this, or what you really desire at all. Notice if doubts arise, and set them aside. Treat this as an experiment in magic, as the spells in one of the most famous grimoires, The Key of Solomon, are labelled. Try it out, make notes, and see what happens.

Whether you find it easy or challenging, sex magic shifts energy and opens you up. Take some time to remind yourself that you choose love and self-care by returning to the, by now familiar, self-love check-in practice.

Take a few minutes to check in with yourself and make a list of three things, as we did in the previous chapters.

1. What do you need right now?
2. What do you desire?
3. What are you grateful for?

Go and do at least one thing you need and one thing you desire. Remember that you are deserving of love and pleasure.

Part IV
Dancing with the Gods

Chapter 9

The Practice of Devotion

Archetypes and Deities of Love and Sex

As witches we dance with the Powers of magic, the forces in the world which shape existence, and in doing so we develop relationships with those Powers. Sometimes we find that they meet us as (or through) powerful, divine, spirit beings; deities.

Some witches work with deities as archetypes, some just tune into the energies behind them, me? I dance with the gods. A devotional relationship with the deities of passion has been a central part of my practice since I began on this path, and, if you'd like to join me, I now extend the hands of invitation.

If you choose to engage with this work as poetic metaphor, then that is also entirely valid, but don't be surprised if They decide to show you things that fall outside of the psychological model.

So far upon this path of crimson craft we have begun to explore our own sacred sexual selves, and the power we can raise to cast spells and conjure our desires, but now we turn to the powers outside of ourselves. My suggestion is that you approach the archetype of The Lover first, and allow for the deities that embody those magics to reveal themselves to you. If, however, you already have a relationship with one or another pantheon or god, then they may already be guiding your journey. Trust your instincts, as always.

Firstly, let's explore the distinction between archetypes and deities, and the metaphysical model in which this particular book is embedded. Which is to say; how does the world of magic work, in your humble author's experience?

When we began in Part I, I spoke of how spirit lives in matter and both are connected. This is where we unpack that together. We understand from our scientific explorations that everything is made of energy, and so, simply put, the different layers of existence are different frequencies, or densities, of energy. If we describe these through the lens of our experience of the world, matter is a denser mass of energy than emotion, which is denser than thought, which is denser than spirit, and so on. These layers can be experienced as "worlds" which overlay each other, and when we shift our attention, our focus, from one layer to another we can experience the ripples of those different worlds. This is what the experience of trance does, it shifts our awareness so we can tune into different frequencies. The reason we can do this is because we exist on each of these levels too. Allow me to demonstrate.

Wherever you are right now, become aware of your body, your physical manifestation.

Take a deep breath and allow your attention to rest in the physical, just noticing how you feel.

On the next breath, allow yourself to relax, and let your attention move to your emotional self.

Breathe with your awareness in the emotional realm, just noticing how you feel emotionally.

When you're ready, on the next breath, allow your attention to drift to your mental self, your thoughts.

Breathe with your awareness here and notice how your thinking self feels.

And when you're ready, on the next breath, allow yourself to relax a little more and let your mind become light.

Allow yourself to become aware of your spirit self.

Breathe with your awareness here, notice how your spirit self feels.

Stay at this point for as long or as short as you like.

And then, when you're ready, breathe deeply, let go of that feeling, and return your attention to your physical self.

Now, each of these aspects of yourself exist in the same space, but at different "frequencies". So too do the layers of reality around you. You can repeat this exercise and, at each stage, notice that part of yourself and then, before you move on, notice that part of the world around you. I recommend doing the "magical practice" from Part II first, however.

Tuning into the Different Worlds

Breathe in. Be aware of your body.
Breathe out. Release tension and relax.
Breathe in. Be aware of the ground.
Breathe out. Send a root of energy into the earth.
Breathe in. Draw up power from the earth into yourself.
With each breath out, send the root deeper.
With each breath in, draw more power up, filling you.
When you are filled with power and rooted deeply...
Breathe out. Send a cord up into the heavens.
Breathe in. Draw starlight down into you, blending with the earth power.
With each breath out, send the cord higher.
With each breath in, draw more power down.
When you are filled with power and connected strongly...
Breathe out. Let the power that fills you expand out into a sphere.
Breathe in. Pull power up from the earth and down from the stars.
Breathe out. As the sphere expands it pushes the etheric dirt from your self.
Breathe in. Fill with more power.
Breathe out. Let the sphere of power surround you as its edges harden into a shield.
Breathe, and become aware of your body again, your physical manifestation.
Take a deep breath and allow your attention to rest in the physical, just noticing how you feel.
Breathe with this awareness of your body, of your bones supporting you upon the earth.
As you breathe allow your attention to expand so you become

aware of the physical world around you.
Breathe with this awareness for a few moments, and then allow
your awareness to return to your body.
On your next breath, allow yourself to relax, and let your
attention move to your emotional self.
Breathe with your awareness in the emotional realm, just noticing
how you feel emotionally.
Slowly allow your attention to expand in the emotional realm, the
feelings of the land upon which you rest.
Breathe with this feeling for a while, before bringing your
awareness back to your emotional self.
When you're ready, on the next breath, allow your attention to
drift to your mental self, your thoughts.
Breathe with your awareness here and notice how your thinking
self feels.
Gradually allow yourself to become aware of the mental realm
around you, the mind of the land about you.
Breathe with this awareness for a little while, and then come back
to your mental self.
And when you're ready, on the next breath, allow yourself to
relax a little more and let your mind become light.
Allow yourself to become aware of your spirit self.
Breathe with your awareness here, notice how your spirit self
feels.
Gently allow your awareness to expand our to the spirit realm,
the spirit of the land where you are.
Stay at this point for as long or as short as you like.
And then, when you're ready, breathe deeply, let go of that
feeling, and allow your awareness to retract to your spirit, and
then gradually shift through your mental self, your emotional
self, and back to your physical self.
When you are ready, open your eyes and move your body. Take
your time returning to everyday consciousness and then, when
you're ready, go and do something grounding.

Marvellous Metaphysics

At this point you may be wondering what this has to do with archetypes and deities. Well, within our world and our lives, we encounter forces, aspects of the world which have an effect on our life and that which is around us, things like gravity, or love. These forces exist in all these different worlds, these many layers of existence, too. At the point where thought and spirit intersect, we have anthropomorphic (or more human appearing) manifestations of these powers.

In my understanding, the thought constructs that we might use to interpret these powers are archetypes, and deities are beings which can carry those archetypes in the spirit realm. So, archetypes are our vision of the roles associated with those Powers, both within ourselves and within the world, and deities are powerful spirit beings who carry those energies and have those roles within their pantheons.

Within magic we can work with those Powers via archetypes, as a mask for us to understand how Sacred Love, for example, might speak with us. Or, we can work with the deities who have their own relationship with Sacred Love, and their own stories to tell about it. In the work we're doing here, we're working with the Power of the Divine Erotic, which can be expressed through the archetypal Lover, and is carried by deities who are known to have a strong affinity for love and sex. As we shall see, those deities are rarely limited to just love and sex, however, and their other attributes shed a light on the power of the Divine Erotic too.

Of course, if you ask a dozen witches to define and describe these things you'll get 13 different answers, so your mileage may vary, but this should give you an idea of how the lines are being drawn in this book. In practice things are much more fluid than categories make them appear but we all need somewhere to begin.

A reminder on gender: In this part of the book there are gendered deities, but I am making no claims that their nature

97

are representative of your gender, or mine, rather that they tell us something about the world we live within more broadly. I invite you to notice how these deities cross the boundaries often ascribed to specific sexes in which attributes they carry. Their stories reflect on our relationship to them culturally, through time and space, and the ways in which they subvert those expectations illustrate how fundamentally beyond modern binary models these beings, and the powers behind them, are. At the same time, there is something of value in the binary model for many people, and thus it continues to have an influence on the way our experience of the divine is expressed, particularly within something so often associated with gender, sex, and sexuality as the erotic.

The Archetypal Lover

The Divine Erotic is the power that flows through this magical path, and the archetype which manifests it is, as you may have guessed, The Lover. Let us now meet the Divine Erotic through the Archetypal Lover, who is also The Beloved. Read through the following text to get an idea of what is involved, and do make any adjustments you need to for your own sense of wellbeing.

Meeting The Lover

Find somewhere comfortable to be and work through the process of the Magical practice from Chapter 5;

Breathe in. Be aware of your body.
Breathe out. Release tension and relax.
Breathe in. Be aware of the ground.
Breathe out. Send a root of energy into the earth.
Breathe in. Draw up power from the earth into yourself.
With each breath out, send the root deeper.
With each breath in, draw more power up, filling you.
When you are filled with power and rooted deeply...

Breathe out. Send a cord up into the heavens.
Breathe in. Draw starlight down into you, blending with the earth
power.
With each breath out, send the cord higher.
With each breath in, draw more power down.
When you are filled with power and connected strongly...
Breathe out. Let the power that fills you expand out into a sphere.
Breathe in. Pull power up from the earth and down from the stars.
Breathe out. As the power expands it pushes the etheric dirt from
your self.
Breathe in. Fill with more power.
Breathe out. Let the sphere of power surround you as its edges harden
into a shield.

Now allow the room beyond your shield to become mist, and as the mist fades you find yourself in a grove of trees, a clearing in a beautiful forest, with a warm fire at the centre and dog roses growing around the circle. Your spirit body here reflects your true self as much as you choose to allow it to. Take a moment to get your bearings and breathe in this space, with the fire and the trees, allowing yourself to hold the intention of meeting The Archetypal Lover.

When you are ready, invite The Lover into the grove. You may choose to use your own words, or the invocation from Chapter 2:

A breath of bliss, caught upon the tongue,
we welcome you, invite you; Divine Lover, come.
Red Goddess dancing, spinning like the sun,
Wild God and Bright Spirit; come, lovers, come.
Bless our hearts, our minds, and skin,
with touch of pleasure welcomed in,
in your honour we begin,
Divine Lover, come!

Into the grove steps The Lover.

They are pleasure incarnate, desire dancing, pure love embodied in delight at the sensual, sensate world. The Lover is that form of sheer joy in being alive, that moment where life is bliss and being flesh is exactly right. Whole and complete unto themselves, The Lover moves through the space like every caress of wind on their skin is the most loving kiss, it is as though they have just eaten their favourite food and their whole face is lit up with the deliciousness of it. Can you recall a time when you felt this way? Or when you noticed a person that you could just tell felt exactly that?

The Lover is a being who embodies bliss. They radiate their enjoyment in their existence like the sun radiates light. There is no expectation of anything, no need for anything more, because right here and now life is just so delightfully pleasurable because it is.

They invite you to come closer, if you choose, and to take their hands.

The sensual power they radiate is gently erotic, there is no demand, but rather they are inviting you to enjoy being sensually alive in your own body. To relax into being alive, present, and awake to the pleasure of embodiment.

Through them also radiates Love, and you can feel it gently washing over and through your heart, offering healing. Perhaps you look upon them and feel Love for them too, and in this way The Lover is also The Beloved, and you, too, are both Beloved and Lover.

Spend as much time here with them as feels right and allow yourself to feel what you need in this moment. You are safe here. When you feel like it is time to return, thank The Lover and bid them farewell. They leave and the mists roll back in, obscuring the grove, and fading to reveal your starting place. Thank them, as you have before:

Lover dear I honour you,
Let your blessings flow,
Know that you are welcome here,
and help my magic grow.
Let me know your sacred ways,
Of love and sex divine,
For now I bid you kind farewell,
You to your home and me to mine.

Breathe into your core for a moment and centre yourself in your body. As you breathe, let the excess power that fills you, any which you do not need, drain away into the earth and sky. Let the sphere of light shrink around you, until you are in your shield, surrounded by light, protected, clean, and energized. Let the connections to earth, sky, and *eros* fade from mind, but know that your root and your cord to the stars are always there, feeding you.

Make any notes in your journal that you feel you would like to remember. Finally, go and do something mundane and grounding, bringing yourself back to everyday consciousness before jumping into the rush of the world if you can.

The Lover may manifest for you as a Divine Androgyne, as a Red Goddess, or as a Wild God. Or perhaps they present as all three at different times, or entirely differently. The way in which they appear to you is a reflection of your relationship to the Divine Erotic power both within yourself and in the world. Notice what this tells you about the power of the Divine Erotic and Love, and what it reveals to you about you.

Uniting with the Beloved

Over time, if you choose, you may repeat this experience of meeting the Lover and, within ritual space, make love with them. If you choose to, ensure that you will be undisturbed, repeat the above journey within ritual space, and allow yourself to be seduced, knowing that this energetic connection is a sharing of love and pleasure, an ecstatic union with the divine. You may choose to touch yourself while you make love together, use sex toys, or simply bask in the feelings that wash over you. Allow yourself to feel what you feel in the long tradition of ecstatic priest/esses and devoted mystics kissed by divine love.

Afterward, be sure to separate fully from them energetically and bring yourself back to yourself. Thank them and bid them farewell before closing your ritual and going to ground yourself.

A Devotional Practice

Not all witches are priests or priestesses, and not all priest/esses (of any gender) are witches. But there is magic in the work of devotion which the witch can use too; theurgy. This is the magic of working with deities, and, here, we can use similar techniques to work with the Powers behind those deities through archetypal beings too, such as *eros* through the Lover-Beloved. If you want to deepen your relationship with any being then there are some universal principles;

Respect

Reciprocation

Time and Attention

Respect for the nature of the being you are approaching is central to building a relationship. If you try to treat them in ways that run counter to their nature then you will run into difficulties. Likewise, being aware of your own boundaries and nature is important too. You get to choose what you will or will not agree to, what is healthy for you, and works with your life. Respect runs both ways.

In any relationship there must also be a sense of reciprocation. You don't need to be getting the same thing out of a friendship as that which you bring to it, but you do need it to feed you in some way, otherwise you will end up drained and resentful. It is the same with spirit relationships. If you only call on these beings when you want something, feeling entitled to it simply because you asked, that is not a good foundation for a relationship.

And any relationship takes time and attention to build. It is possible to treat deities like experts for hire, and many people do, but as witches who are working towards healthy relationships, working with the powers of love and sex, that is not the kind of interaction we are seeking with our gods and the Powers behind them.

You may also find yourself considering the notions of worship and devotion. Worship has, at its root, the idea of treating a being as *worthy* of devotion and attention, and perhaps of increasing your worthiness through that attention. It is an offering of love, which often includes a reciprocation of love from the deity in question, or, if not love, then blessings of another kind. Devotion is perhaps a deeper level of worship; it is a commitment. Whether a commitment to a being or an ideal, when we are devoted to something we give it attention and support it, encouraging its presence and increase in the world.

Reflecting On The Beloved

What makes a good relationship between beings?
How does working with deity feel to you?
What does respect mean to you?
How do you feel about the concepts of worship and devotion?

A relationship with *eros*, with the Divine Lover-Beloved, or with a deity of passion, then, is built on respect, reciprocity, time and attention. Over time it may deepen from building connection, to worship, through to devotion. But there is no need to rush this process, or to go any further along that particular path than is right for you. Devotion is far from the only magical path, and it is neither the only goal nor the most valuable choice. If it is where your heart is led, however, then here is a good place to begin. Here are some ways of building a foundational relationship with The Beloved, or the Power or deity of your choosing.

Stories

Begin to collect stories and poetry about The Beloved. This is especially important when working with deities of particular cultures as it helps you to tune into them specifically, but The Lover-Beloved has had many beautiful pieces penned in their honour. Read them aloud to yourself, or listen to recordings of them. Feel the vibrations in your body. Mull over the imagery and emotions. Get to know them through the words already in the world about them

Shrines

As you created an altar in Chapter 6, this is a similar process except that the purpose of a shrine is to offer a home for The Beloved. Choose visual, tactile, and sensual representations of them, and that you feel they would like. You may begin by simply laying out a cloth of a colour that makes sense to you, black or white as neutral colours, or red for love and passion perhaps, in a space which can slowly be decorated and filled as you come to understand them better. You may find that objects which would be suitable start to find their way to you, as The Beloved sends you gifts and ways to help them feel more at home there. Art of them is a good choice. The shrine is also a good space to make prayers and leave offerings. If it is suitable, then a candle, to light when you are communing with them, is a useful centre piece.

Offerings

Offerings are gifts of energy and love, offered to strengthen the being they are given to, and the relationship. Just like you would offer a guest a drink when they visit your home, so too is it worthwhile offering The Beloved sustenance. Pouring them a drink, lighting incense, or even offering them a song or poem or other creative expression are all things that can work well. You may have found things in the stories which would make suitable offerings – though please do ensure that they are legal and ethical, the old tales can sometimes be a little bloodthirsty! Honey, strawberries, chocolate, or foods seen as aphrodisiacs may be worth trying within the work we do. If you are giving food or drink as an offering, you may want a dish as part of the shrine to put the offerings into. Remember to dispose of them before they go mouldy or get snaffled by pets, 24 hours is usually plenty of time. When you do, consider how you might choose to get rid of it safely. Dark chocolate can be highly toxic to wildlife, so while you might choose to pour wine out in the garden, that is not recommended for chocolate cookies. One option is to offer the spirit of the item to The Beloved, and ask that they bless what they leave behind for you to eat, so you are sharing a feast together, such as may happen in Hindu pujas.

Prayers
Prayers can be very simple, or highly elaborate. There are traditional prayers to many deities which you can read, learn, or be inspired by. You may choose to collect your favourites in your grimoire. But, the simplest, heartfelt greetings in your own words are very powerful. Spend time at your shrine, light a candle and incense, or an equivalent, and speak with The Beloved. Greet them, tell them why you're there and what you're seeking. Ask them questions if you choose to. And listen. Feel for their presence, and maybe their response.

Divination
You can also communicate with the divine through divination, such as oracle decks, tarot, runes, or scrying in smoke, flame,

water, or sound. Scrying can be a very useful way of calming your mind to allow for you to feel their response.

To scry you need a focal point. Traditional ones include those already mentioned, such as a candle flame, but you can also choose a steady sound, like that of a singing bowl or rain, the reflection of your own pupils in the mirror, or a sensation, such as drawing circles on your palm with a fingertip or feather. The important aspect of whichever you choose is its consistency.

Set your attention to connect with The Beloved.

~ Allow your breathing to become slow and steady and bring it to focus on the point you have chosen.
~ Breathe through the layers of attention as you did at the start of this chapter and let your awareness rest at the level of spirit.
~ Gently allow your spirit-attention to expand, keeping your conscious mind occupied with the scrying focus point.
~ Allow yourself to notice The Beloved near, and any messages they have for you.

When you are ready, thank them and allow your attention to retract, coming back to the point of your spirit body, then back to your physical self, and finally returning to where you began.

Make notes and then do something mundane and grounding, like eating salty snacks, or housework.

Practice

Whichever pieces you choose to use in your relationship building, start small and build up slowly. Be honest with yourself about how much time and attention you have, or can make, to do this work. If you can only set aside one evening a month, then dedicate that time to this practice. You may build up to doing more in the future, or you may find you end up doing a bigger ritual each time, but only once every season. This is your relationship with The Beloved, and it must work for you, but need not look like anyone else's relationship with them. This is why it is a devotional *practice*. It is something you do, rather than an ideal of perfection which never happens.

When the Holy Maiden Comes

Slipping, with a tender smile,
'Tween bone and flesh and
shining, all the while
she takes me... elsewhere.
Deep within the circle bright,
the Horned One moves,
conducting the song of night,
with sure hands and dancing hooves.
Blessed, are we, to witness this,
Star maiden and horned one,
power rises from their kiss,
healing flows when the gods come.

Self-Love Check-In

How are you feeling? Has anything excited or unsettled you in this chapter? What might that tell you about yourself? Crafting a devotional practice is a slow process, and working with those archetypes can rub up against old wounds, if that is the case for you, then as always, I invite you to practice self-care and to continue cultivating your expressions of self-love.

Take some time now, then, to remind yourself that you choose love and self-care by returning to the, by now familiar, self-love check-in practice.

Take a few minutes to check in with yourself and make a list of three things, as we did in the previous chapters.

1. What do you need right now?
2. What do you desire?
3. What are you grateful for?

Go and do at least one thing you need and one thing you desire. Remember that you are deserving of love and pleasure.

Chapter 10

The Erotic Divinities

Once Lilith Came
Once,
you showed me a little black serpent.
It slid through the dirt
writing its love of the land
in the tracks left behind.
Its scales stroking
the earth
with every motion,
a lover
who could not bear to be parted
from the object
of their devotion.

Once,
you had me listen to the owls
calling in the night
from the tall trees that stay green
into the depths of winter.
Their voices echoed
off the valley walls
and they spoke to each other
unafraid
of the darkness
that hid my watchful eyes
and held them safe.

Once,
you lifted my feet from the ground

with your strong winds
and let me feel like I could fly
just for a moment.

Once,
you slipped into my bed,
your fingers softly insistent
that my body was as worthy of touch
as the earth.
Your voice was enchanting,
summoning cries of pleasure in the darkness,
reminding me that
it is safe to be heard.
You moved me that night,
lifting me
from the mistaken belief
that I was asking for too much.

Once,
you dancing through my life
woke my body
touched my mind
kissed my soul
and gave me back my heart.
Pure and whole and mine
to choose what I desire.

Red Goddesses

Some say it was a serpent, some say it was Lilith Herself,
the first woman, who offered humanity knowledge.
Knowledge of good and evil, pleasure and pain.
People say a lot of things.
Sometimes they're right.

Magic. Sex. War. Love. The deities of passion hold all these things in their grasp. The Goddesses of Passion are known by many names and many faces.

Inanna, Aphrodite, Lilith, Freyja, Venus, Babalon...

Each one of these goddesses is a deity of love, sex, war and magic, all at once. They hold passion in their blood, a heat that flows through all they do. They are whole, sovereign over their own lives, whatever challenges they undergo as they face the darkness or seek their desires.

Lady of Desire.
Queen of Heaven,
Blessed are the lips that speak your names.

Love and righteous war are two sides of the same coin, both involve desire and boundaries, whether invoking or dissolving. Sex and magic are two sides of the same coin too; both driven by desire, by need, and fuelled by the flow of life-force. Sex and magic, just like love and war, both create and transform. If the idea of war being tied to sex, love, and magic, concerns you, do not think of soldiers and modern warfare. Think of warriors instead, seeking to defend that which they love, or win what they need, for themselves and for their community. Now think of both the passion of violence and the letting go of control in orgasm. Spend some time knowing that the Goddesses of Love hold fighting, magic, and sex together as expressions of passion, when guided by honour these are all powerful things. Hold this knowing in your mind, in your heart, and allow the understanding that it offers to rise. If you are uncomfortable with any of these four, ask yourself why.

Within each of us is the capacity for love, for passion, for desire, for violence – even if only in defence – and for magic.

Accepting these possibilities in ourselves allows us to both find peace, and tap into the power that is so often wasted in fighting our own natures. We can then choose how to use these parts of ourselves with honour. The Queen of Heaven can help guide us in finding and accepting these parts of ourselves, and in learning how to channel them.

There is a tendency to equate love with self-sacrifice, and sometimes that is right, but these ladies stand tall in the circle of their own power, in the power of love, and demonstrate that love can also be self-strengthening.

What is Love?

It is a good question to ponder; what is love? Why is it that the goddesses of love, such as Freya, Aphrodite, Inanna, are so often warrior goddesses too? Perhaps because love is a passion, love is a feeling that fills one with fire. Whether that fire is the gentle hearth or the roaring bonfire, it is akin to the fire that can be used to protect the ones we love from darkness. Or perhaps it is because loving someone or something means being willing to protect them. And that includes one's self. The goddesses of love know their boundaries, they are fiercely protective of the ones they love, and they shine that bright light of love on their own selves. Love is not self-sacrifice; it is being wholly ones' selves with each other.

Too many narratives speak of love as pain. But I don't buy it. Loss hurts, betrayal and rejection hurt. But love? Love is what lifts us up and fills our hearts with joy. Love is caring so much that you only want the subject of your love to be happy, healthy, whole. Love is feeling better in yourself for that which you love being in your life.

This is why love in a relationship works best when you cultivate self-love alongside love-for-other; because we each need to bring our whole, authentic selves to life in order to be all we can be. The goddesses of love know this, and that is why so many of their devotees today advocate for self-love.

A Reflection; Love is...

For this reflection I recommend doing this as an automatic writing exercise. For automatic writing the trick is to set a timer (or a number of pages) and to the write for the whole time allotted without allowing yourself to think too much about what you are writing. Let whatever comes out come out onto the page. If you get stuck, write out the prompt statement or question until you find the next words spilling from you. You can do this after grounding, centring, and connecting to the earth and sky as in the magical practice from Chapter 5, or a similar practice to calm your mind and bring yourself to the present moment. If writing is hard, this can also be done through typing or speaking into a voice recorder.

Turn to a fresh page and begin with the prompt; "Love is..." write for five minutes.

"I can love myself more by..."

Look back over what you have written and highlight any patterns or key phrases. Notice what you have written and what that tells you about your relationship toward love. Once you have finished exploring this, ask yourself;

What is one thing you will do today that helps you feel more whole, more at peace, more loved? How are you going to honour the goddesses of love, and their magic in yourself, today? Write down any ideas you have and then pick one thing that feels good to do now.

Wild Gods

When pagans ask about the deities of love and sex, more often than not we'll hear about goddesses, and it's telling that the gods of passion are not as well talked about as the goddesses. Perhaps because we have been encouraged to be scared of masculine sexuality. Or perhaps the goddess movement has been reclaiming the divine embodied nature as it manifests in the feminine for the past half century or so, and now, in our Western world, we simply still have work to do, to do the same for our gods. There are so many twists and turns to our history that the reasons are less important than the work ahead; remembering the gods of love and lust, not just as consorts but as powerful, wonderful beings in their own right.

Cernunnos still dances in the wildwood, and Pan's pipes are calling, and Frey still blesses the land with his golden glow and large... *ehem*... member. Our gods of passion, of love and lust and pleasure, still walk with us. The god Eros with his bow may be reduced in popular imagination to the little cupids on Valentine's Day cards but the power of love is still as strong as ever.

But passion is a scary thing. It leaves up open to danger, and makes us more inclined to take risks. And as we've seen with the warrior aspects of the goddesses, passion isn't limited to love and lust, but can also include violence. The conflation of these two scares people away from erotic expressions, especially from the masculine.

I say; *enough of that*.

Each one of us, regardless of gender, has to learn to temper our passions, and to know when to let them pour out into the world. And so, the gods of love are so often depicted as wild and kind in equal measure, they are both hunters and protectors of life, with their passions held in balance in service of their love. And here is the lesson of the gods of passion; where the goddesses can teach us about boundaries of self, the gods can teach us about boundaries of community and family. Passion is both expression and protection, and is this not love?

What we love, we care for.

And those we love; we welcome into the circle of our family. Into our protection.

Remembering this, can we perhaps see that this applies to

sexuality too? And that limiting ourselves to one narrow model of eroticism, one vision of masculine sexuality, harms everyone bound by it? Could it be better if we meet, instead, as people. As individuals in the circle of passion and relate, heart-to-heart?

In the same way we have been denied the personal power in pleasure and our own bodily autonomy by being punished and pressured to conform to arbitrary limitations, we have also been scared away from passion through its association with violence. And sometimes that passion becomes violence because it has no healthy outlet.

Perhaps we might turn to Frey, to the kind, gentle lord of the Alfar who protects the land, loves his wife, and embodies the virility of lust. In Frey we can learn of an alternative to the negative model of toxic masculinity which is, yes, acted out by some and used to keep many of us scared of passion. Frey is not reduced to merely a consort but he is rather a powerful god in his own right, and he channels his passion for the benefit of the land, the community, and his family, with and for love. Perhaps with his guidance more men can find a role model for healthy passion, and people who love men can learn to recognise those that embody healthy expressions of love.

See, here, the balance of boundaries and care, the protection of that which is loved. And so it is with all the gods of passion, our gods of the wild.

A Reflection; Learning to Trust Ourselves

To explore where you may have come to be scared of your own power and passion, set aside some time for automatic writing, as in the previous reflection. In your journal ask yourself the question; how do I trust in my power, my strength, my passion?

Give yourself five minutes and just write without stopping on the ways in which you trust your power.

"I trust in my power, strength, and passion..."

Now do the same again, writing for five minutes in answer to the question; how do I *not* trust my power, my strength, my passion?

"I do not trust in my power, strength, and passion..."

Finally, ask yourself; how can I learn to trust my strength, my power, my passion more?
Write for five minutes.

"I can trust in my power, strength, and passion more by..."

Look over what you have written. What do you notice? You may choose to highlight certain phrases or thoughts that jump out at you. What does this tell you about yourself-trust and your comfort with your own strength, power, and passion? What suggestions have you just given yourself? You can repeat this with each of the concepts separately, writing for five minutes on your strength, then your power, then your passion. Look over what you've written again. How are these things connected to you? How are they different?

If there is a part of your divine erotic self which you are scared to accept because you have been taught to distrust your own power and passion, consider if there is a step you can take today. Perhaps you can consider making a commitment to yourself to accept that part of yourself simply as part of you.

Bright Spirits

Star Goddess, Blue God, Great Spirit, Lover, Beloved...

And then... and then... The Queer, Bright Spirits. The deities of love and lust and passion who are not simply male nor female, who are not limited to binaries but flow between possibilities and expression. The deities that sit in that strange space which modern English so often forgets to name. Them, the Divine Queer Spirits, the ergi and transformative and limitless.

We have the Feri Star Goddess, God Hirself, the pre-gendered divine ground of Being, and Their manifest, multigendered expression in the Blue God. We have Hermaphroditus, the union or child of Aphrodite and the Messenger, Hermes; he who moves between. We have Spirit, ungendered and all gendered. We have the crossdressing and sex-changing deities in myths, Baphomet, the primal androgyne, and the pure bright spirit that is simply "Lover", other, outside of the language I have to offer.

The deities of love and liminality are, like many historically who walked between the more common binary roles of "man" and "woman", in an especially powerful place for weaving magic as that which moves between the worlds. Theirs' is the mystery of love; its transcendence and power.

And there is more besides. Many deities we describe as male or female are also known for their fluidity and ability to transcend those human boundaries. Loki is both Mother of Sleipnir and Father of the World Serpent, among others. Inanna is named in an ancient prayer as having the power to grant her followers the ability to transform between genders, and is said to have been worshipped by cross-dressing or transgendered priest/esses. Venus, as Venus Barbata, grew a beard to court a gay man, Aphrodite is sometimes depicted as a hermaphrodite as Aphroditus, Frey "gave up his sword" for love, and as we explore the myths of cultures across the world there are many hints, and outright statements, that many deities are not limited to one sex or gender expression.

The gods are often as queer and fluid as they are masculine or feminine. Here, then, is a mystery of acceptance and fluidity, and of the nature of potential. All are expressions of the vastness of magic, and of life.

Reflection; Dancing with Spirit

As before, prepare yourself for automatic writing by getting comfortable and grounding, centring, and connecting to the divine within the earth and sky. Take up your journal and set your timer for five minutes. Begin your automatic writing with the prompt;

"I cross categories because..."

Next write for five minutes on;

"I am unlimited because..."

Finally, write for five minutes on;

"The Divine is unlimited because..."

Look back over what you have written. What do you notice? How do you feel? Spend a little time just being present with whatever you have uncovered.

Self-Love Check-In

How are you feeling after this chapter? Has anything excited or unsettled you in this chapter? What might that tell you about yourself? The Deities of Passion, the Goddesses, Gods, and Bright Spirits each have powerful lessons for us. As you have probably noticed by now, I highly recommend checking back in with yourself and rooting your magic in being your own Beloved. Here again is our practice for just that. Take some time now, to remind yourself that you choose love and self-care by returning to the, by now familiar, self-love check-in.

Take a few minutes to check in with yourself and make a list of three things, as we did in the previous chapters.

1. What do you need right now?
2. What do you desire?
3. What are you grateful for?

Go and do at least one thing you need and one thing you desire. Remember that you are deserving of love and pleasure.

Chapter 11

The Deities of Passion

Working with Deities

This chapter includes *very* brief descriptions of some of the deities of passion and their major myths. If any of these are calling to you then this can act as a jumping off point. Take a look in Chapter 9 for tips on building a devotional practice, and explore the information there on building altars, praying, divination as a method of communication, and so on, to inspire you.

From here, find the myths and stories of the deities who you are drawn to, if any, and spend time learning about their history, culture, and modern expressions. There are communities and groups devoted to every deity you can think of, and joining one is a good way to find further resources, and to hear stories of how people are experiencing and honouring them today. You do not have to work with deity at all, but if you choose to, I wish you every blessing upon your dance with them ahead.

Alongside a brief introduction to each deity, I have included a magical *working* which you might like to do if you are drawn to work with them, or to tune into some of the energies which each are commonly associated with. These are not historical rituals or spells, but are rather practices for you to explore. As always, you may choose to use the ritual opening and closing outlined in the appendix, based on the magical practices which we have worked with throughout this book, or you may prefer to use another method of preparing yourself and creating sacred space.

The symbolism and imagery listed may be useful as a starting point for building a shrine to the deity you are working with, if you so desire. There is some overlap between each of the deities here as they often share roots and are dealing with similar energies. Those similarities may point to something about *eros*, the power of sex, love, and passion which belongs to all of the deities listed.

I have presented each of these workings with the deity that suggested them to me, but you may find that one deity calls to you, and is happy to work with some or all of the other workings too, perhaps with adaptations. Allow your relationship with them to evolve and see what happens in your working together.

Explore, expand, and keep notes of what you discover works for you and your devotional practice.

Freya

Freya is the Vanadis, golden Goddess of the Heathens. She is described as the most beautiful (and lusted after) goddess in the Nine Worlds. She is independent, noted as having many lovers of her own choosing, and of teaching the ancient magic of Seidr. She is sometimes considered to be the leader of the warrior maidens and psychopomps known as the Valkyries, and half of those slain in battle are chosen to live in her great hall after death. Freya and her brother Frey were originally part of the tribe of the Vanir, deities who seem to have been associated with fertility and agriculture, and as such she carries that vitality in her. Her chariot is pulled by two Northern wildcats, she owns a cloak of feathers which can transform the wearer into a hawk, and her magical necklace, Brísingamen, is an object of power and beauty. Freya, then, is the Mistress of Magic, goddess of sex and beauty, as well as magic and death, a powerful warrior, and just generally pretty gorgeous.

Symbolism and Imagery

Gold
Amber
Honey, or honey-mead
Cats (especially European wildcats)

Hooded cloaks
Falcons and their feathers
Jewellery

A Working; Recognising your Power with Freya

For this working you will want an oracle of your choosing such as runes or a tarot deck.

Before the working, gather either a selection of beads and a thread to string them upon to make a necklace; or a piece of string or cord in red, gold, or a colour of your choosing; or paper and pen, pencil, or art supplies.

~ Prepare yourself and your space for ritual.

~ Perform the ritual opening of your choosing and place an offering to Freya on your altar.

~ Invite Freya to be present and to guide your working here.

~ Spend some time noticing what her presence feels like.

~ Sit with her for a while and then, with your oracle to hand, ask Freya about the road ahead on this journey for you. You might ask about what you need to do next to support your relationship with her, or your journey in sexual magic. You may ask about how to find the confidence within yourself to express your whole beautiful self. You may have other questions to ask.

~ Ask, and ask what she'd like in return for her guidance in finding your own sexual power.

~ Negotiate until whatever you agree to is both something you are happy to do, and a commitment you are capable of fulfilling.

~ Now, take the beads and thread them onto the string, knotting it after each one if you can. With each bead, ask her to name it for one of your gifts, a way in which you are powerful, beautiful, sexy. Notice how you feel, what is she pointing out to you. Use your oracle if you like. Once you feel confident, name the bead aloud yourself as you knot the thread.

~ If you do not have beads, place knots along the cord and name each knot for your gifts.

~ If you have brought art supplies instead, then draw your necklace, naming each bead as you draw them.

~ When you have finished your necklace of power and beauty, place it on your altar or around your neck and notice how you feel, blessed and powerful.

~ Spend as long as you like here, you may choose to do some further divination, to read one of her stories, to compose a bawdy love song to her, or to just meditate with her until it is time to close.

~ Thank Freya and perform your ritual closing.

~ Make any notes you need to and ground yourself by doing something mundane.

Continue to honour her and build on your relationship over time with offerings, maintaining a shrine for her, and learning about her stories. Remember to fulfil the commitment you have made.

Aphrodite

In Hesiod's version of events, it is said that Aphrodite was born of the ocean foam, arising when Chronos (time) castrated Ouranos (The Sky) and threw his genitals into the sea. She is often described as Aphroditus Ourania, Aphrodite the Heavenly, and her lineage reaches back through Astarte, to Ishtar, and back to Inanna, and it is no surprise that the Romans syncretised Aphrodite with Venus, goddess of beauty and love. Aphrodite has deep roots. She is a powerful Lady, lustful and passionate and her retinue, the Erotes, winged gods of love and lust who include the god Eros, indicates her lineage manifesting in action. Her many epithets show a variety of faces, and from "Smile-loving" to "Gravedigger" she encompasses the bright and dark powers of both love and death. And of course, she sometimes appears as Aphroditus, depicted in sculpture as bearded, breasted, in a dress, flashing their phallus and all its lusty, virile, luck at the viewer. Aphrodite is known to be generous to her followers, and vengeful to those that wrong her.

Symbolism and Imagery

Pink and red, or white and blue for the ocean
Sea shells
"Venus on a half-shell" paintings
Hand Mirrors
Pearls
Roses
Doves

A Working; Honouring Beauty with Aphrodite

Ensure you have a hand mirror on your altar. You may also want to acquire some rose water, or something similarly scented, for this working.

~ Prepare yourself and your space for ritual.
~ Perform the ritual opening of your choosing and place an offering to Aphrodite on your altar.
~ Invite Aphrodite to join you, in all her glorious beauty.
~ Spend some time basking in her presence and feeling it reflecting upon you. Allow yourself to adore her as befits such a beauty. Request her blessing, that you may know both your own beauty and hers.
~ When you are ready, pick up the mirror.

~ Allow the mirror to reflect back energetically the beauty that you hold inside you.
~ Feel this reflection.
~ If you can, begin to hum or sing, and allow the mirror to reflect the wonder of your voice back to you.
~ Whichever senses are suitable for you at this time, allow the mirror to show you the beauty that Aphrodite calls from you with her blessing.
~ If you like, wet your hands with rose water and breathe in its scent. You can ask Aphrodite to bless the bottle if you choose.
~ Spend as long as you like here, you may choose to continue basking in the divine beauty within yourself and the goddess, to do some divination, to read one of her stories or devotional poetry to her or Venus, or to just meditate with her until it is time to close.
~ Thank Aphrodite and perform your ritual closing.
~ Make any notes you need to and ground yourself by doing something mundane.

Continue to honour her with offerings and by maintaining her shrine, and in the ways which make sense to you. Whenever you work with her, anoint yourself with the rose water and allow its scent to remind you of the divine beauty.

The Blue God

The Blue God is a figure who dances through cultures and spaces, virile and vibrant life made beautiful, dancing life and death. Depicted as powerfully masculine, but containing the expression of fluidity that allows him to be beyond confinement. The Blue God is the Dancing God, expressing life joyfully and proud, power flowing through him freely. In Feri Witchcraft he is named Dian Y Glas, and is youthful, vibrant, shimmering like the sky. Through his connection with the Peacock Angel who originated with the Yezidi people, he is the first shining light of the Divine, and knows his worth and power.

Symbolism and Imagery

Peacocks and peacock feathers
Storms
Blue
Mirrors
Dancing figures
Bells

A Working; Pride and Self-Acceptance with The Blue God

Before this working, spend a little time reflecting on how comfortable you are with being proud of yourself and your accomplishments. You may wish to journal on this.

~ Prepare yourself and your space for ritual.
~ Perform the ritual opening of your choosing and place an offering to The Blue God on your altar.
~ Invite him to join you in your ritual.
~ Allow yourself to relax with your breathing and to feel his presence with you.
~ Feel life flowing within you, that spark of power that you are.
~ Feel his pride in you.
~ And allow yourself to feel pride in yourself, just as you are now.
~ Allow yourself to gently move with this feeling, whether just with your breath or all the way up to dancing with your whole body. Move with your pride, with his pride in you. Move as you are, whole and complete

and worthy. Allow him to show you how it feels to be worthy, because you are.

~ Spend as long as you like dancing with him, or you may choose to do some divination, to toast to him beauty and yours, or to just meditate with him until it is time to close.

~ Thank The Blue God and perform your ritual closing.

~ Make any notes you need to and ground yourself by doing something mundane.

Continue to build your relationship with him over time with prayers, maintaining a shrine, making offerings, or whatever feels right to do.

Lilith

Lilith was an ancient Spirit, in Hebrew folklore often considered to be the first wife of Adam, before Eve. Some interpret both Adam (as the being split to give rise to Eve) and Lilith (as a feminine being who is described with masculine attributes, and who refused to be subservient to Adam) as originally being hermaphrodite-beings, containing all the potential of humanity within them.

The story goes that Lilith refused to lie beneath Adam and chose instead to travel the world as an independent being, becoming mother to thousands through her own choice. Some say it was Lilith that tempted Eve into eating of the tree of knowledge, perhaps teaching her that there was more than obedience, but others would disagree.

The earliest mentions of Lilith place her as a spirit of the wind, and describe her as a kind of succubus. Today some approach her as a goddess who knows her own mind and chooses independence, freedom, and pleasure, honouring her own needs above the demands of convention.

Symbolism and Imagery

Owls (especially the screech owl)
Goat legs
Apples
A black serpent
The Dark Moon
Black and silver

A Working; Choosing Yourself with Lilith

This working is best performed naked, if possible, so make sure you have a warm enough space, and a blanket or comfortable clothes to hand for afterward.

Have some anointing oil, red wine, or water to hand for anointing yourself with.

~ Prepare yourself and your space for ritual.
~ Perform the ritual opening of your choosing and place an offering to Lilith on your altar.
~ Call to Lilith. Ask her to show to you how to choose yourself.
~ Call to her and just be, in your circle, with her.
~ Listen to her.
~ Feel her around you.
~ Feel her power to choose for herself reflected in you.
~ When you have a feeling of what it would feel like to have that power yourself, anoint yourself on your forehead, heart, and just above your genitals saying at each point; I am divine. I am whole. I choose me
~ Notice how the energy shifts and be present with yourself and Lilith.
~ You may, at this point, choose to share an apple with Lilith, placing half upon the altar as an offering and

eating half yourself, savouring its sweetness.
~ Spend as long as you like here, you may choose to do some divination, to read one of her stories, or to just meditate with her until it is time to close.
~ Thank Lilith and perform your ritual closing.
~ Make any notes you need to and ground yourself by doing something mundane and cleaning up if you need to.

You may choose to build the relationship if it feels right by making regular offerings, maintaining a shrine, or by fiercely choosing your own path and to honour your own needs and, each time, saying a prayer of your own choosing in honour of Lilith. Just be aware that relationships often require a certain amount of compromise, and she tends to discourage that when it might be detrimental to what you actually want, and that can sometimes have a negative impact on human relationships. Conversely, sometimes, that energy can be exactly what we need.

Cernunnos

Cernunnos is an ancient antlered god, found in Celtic imagery and named for his antlers. He is literally "the Horned God". Cernunnos is usually depicted as seated, cross-legged, surrounded by animals, and often with a hunting horn. He is often associated with chthonic, underworld powers, and the movement between worlds. His antlers and animalistic legs show his connections to the primal, animal realm, as well as perhaps reaching between the upper world (with his antlers) and down into the underworld (his hooves). As such Cernunnos may be the ultimate mediator between the worlds, fully balancing his material and divine nature with compassion.

Symbolism and Imagery

Antlers or horns
Hunting horn
Horned/antlered figures
Forest animals, particularly the stag
Bow and arrows
Hunting knife

A Working; Honouring the Animal Self with Cernunnos

You may wish to have a steady drum beat playing for this ritual,
or to be playing a steady beat on a drum or rattle yourself.

~ Prepare yourself and your space for ritual.

~ Perform the ritual opening of your choosing and place
an offering to Cernunnos on your altar. Invite him to join
you and guide you in tuning into your own animal self.
Imagine a deep forest surrounding you through which
he arrives.

~ Spend some time soaking up his presence and breathing
with him, listening and communing with him.

~ Ask him to guide you in honouring him and your own
sacred animal nature.

~ Rest in this space and allow the knowing of your own
animal self, here, today, in this ritual, to arise within you.

~ Under Cernunnos' guidance, begin to feel what it would
be like to be the archetype of that animal.

~ Feel your spirit self tune into the shape of that animal
and allow yourself to move as that animal, as much
as you are able and comfortable doing so. Spend time
exploring what it feels like to be a sacred animal, under
his protection.

~ Notice what he is like when you are animal, and if that

feels different to when you are human.

~ Spend as long as you like here, you may choose to do some divination, to further commune with your animal self, or to just meditate with Cernunnos until it is time to close.

~ When you are ready, choose to return to human consciousness, becoming aware of your human shape. Thank Cernunnos and the animals that have guided you today and perform your ritual closing.

~ Make any notes you need to and ground yourself by doing something mundane.

You might choose to add a representation of your animal self to your shrine to Cernunnos, or to make a mask or costume to explore and integrate that part of you further in future rituals. Repeat this working as many times as you like to deepen your relationship with him and yourself. Build your relationship with him in the ways that make sense to you, perhaps with offerings, or perhaps with visits to forests or old oak trees in the parks nearby.

Frey

Frey is the golden god of the Heathens. Brother to Freya, he too is of the Vanir, the divine tribe of fertility and growth, and was also sent as a willing hostage to be part of the peace-deal between the tribes of the gods. It is said that he fell in love with a beautiful giantess, Gerda, who was tending her garden and would only agree to marry him if he gave his magical sword to her family, so that when the peace ended and the world was destroyed and remade in Ragnarök, Frey had only an antler to fight with and his power was given over to the giants, who can be seen as the primal forces of nature personified. Frey chose love and gave his sword to her family, and he and Gerda are said to be very devoted to one another. Frey is also described as the

Lord of Alfheim, home of the Alfar, who are both described as Elves and as male ancestors.

Frey is known as a good leader, as he comes from a place of peacekeeping, of love, and of helping the world to grow. His approach is thus one of support and care. Some sources also describe his worship as involving a large horse phallus, and cross-dressers dancing with bells on their ankles in his honour, suggesting that pleasure and celebration are important to this god, which I have found is certainly the case.

Symbolism and Imagery

Gold
Horses
An antler
A large phallus
A growing potted plant (for his love of Gerda)
A boat
Wheat or ripe grain plants
The sun

A Working; Sacrifice for Love with Frey

Before this working take some time to reflect, and journal if you wish, on the concept of self-sacrifice, boundaries, and compromise.

~ Prepare yourself and your space for ritual.
~ Perform the ritual opening of your choosing and place an offering to Frey on your altar.
~ Invite Frey to join you and spend some time with him, feel his presence and imagine he is there to talk to you. What might he tell you about sacrifice for love and peace? About devotion and protection of that which is important to you?

~ Contemplate the life of plants grown for grain; how they rise up and are cut down, how they die to spread their seeds and support their family. You may also contemplate the sacrifices that your ancestors may have made that have allowed you to be here now, whether they are ancestors of your bloodline, or ancestors of culture.

~ And perhaps you might like to ask yourself; What have you sacrificed for love? What is worth sacrificing for love? And what is not worth sacrificing?

~ When is it good to fight, and when is it good to choose peace?

~ Listen to what Frey might have to share with you.

~ Spend as long as you like here, you may choose to do some divination, to read one of his stories, or to just meditate with him until it is time to close.

~ Thank Frey and perform your ritual closing.

~ Make any notes you need to and ground yourself by doing something mundane.

Continue to build your relationship with him over time with prayers, maintaining a shrine, making offerings, or whatever you are drawn to do for him.

Inanna

Inanna is a 7000 (or more) year old Sumerian goddess, later known as Ishtar, who gave rise to the lineage of sex, love, and war deities that came after her. She was known as the Queen of Heaven, and was very determined to gain as much power as she could. She tricked the god Enki into giving her the *mes*, various divine powers for maintaining the divine order. She is still well known for the rather explicit hymn talking about the love (and lust) between her and the shepherd, Dumuzid, who she eventually marries. But her most famous myth is that of her descent into the underworld, Kur. Inanna decides to go to Kur and dresses in all her most powerful items. There are seven gates she must pass through before reaching her sister, Ereshkigal, in her throne room, and at each the gatekeeper Neti strips her of an item until she is finally naked and powerless. Despite this, she sits on her sister's throne and, for this arrogance, is struck dead. Inanna had left a back-up plan in place and, as a result, she is eventually rescued and returned to her throne in the heavens, and her husband takes her place in Kur.

Inanna knows her worth, and the resources at her disposal. She trusts in her power to get her out of trouble, and she seeks more. She fully embraces her nature as a sexual being. Her hymns show that she knows how to love and be loved, the importance of pleasure, and how to ask for what she needs and desires.

Symbolism and Imagery

Gold
Lapiz lazuli
Lions
The eight pointed star
Venus (the planet)

A Working; Claiming your Power with Inanna

Before the ritual, acquire a scarf or cloth in a colour which represents power to you, and decide on something you can do daily for seven days as an offering to Inanna, such as saying her name each morning and evening, lighting a candle in her honour, burning incense, or pouring a fresh offering at her shrine.

~ Prepare yourself and your space for ritual.
~ Perform the ritual opening of your choosing and place an offering to Inanna on your altar.
~ Invite Inanna to join you for this working and to guide you.

~ Place your power-item before you.

~ Breathe deeply and allow your eyes to close.

~ Feel Inanna there with you. Spend a little time in her presence.

~ If you wish, state your intention to honour her and know her better.

~ Notice how you feel her respond.

~ When you are ready, begin to pay attention to how you feel in yourself. Contemplate the ways in which you feel powerful, and the ways in which you feel powerless.

~ Consider your scarf. Hold it in your hands.

~ Ask Inanna to bless it with the strength and courage to claim your personal divine erotic power, in return for the seven days of honouring her in the way you have decided.

~ Feel her response, and her blessing on the scarf.

~ When it feels right, put it on and notice how you feel different.

~ Spend as long as you like here, you may choose to do some divination, to read one of Inanna's stories or hymns, or to just meditate with her until it is time to close.

~ Thank Inanna and perform your ritual closing.

~ Make any notes you need to and ground yourself by doing something mundane.

Remember to perform the daily piece you have committed to for the next seven days. After this time, you can continue to honour Inanna with offerings, study, and maintaining her shrine, or in other ways which will become clear to you over time.

Baphomet

Baphomet is an iconic winged goat-headed image with both breasts and a phallic rod often used as a representation or symbol of the devil, but the use of this image for the being that epitomizes the synthesis of apparent opposites finds its roots in alchemy and occultism. The name Baphomet was found in the trials of the Knights Templar over a thousand years ago, presented as a heresy, but the being we know today takes its visage from illustrations of the "sabbatic goat" by Éliphas Lévi, in other words, the focal point of magical work in ecstatic witchcraft, mistaken for the devil but actually representing the manifestation of all that is.

Including Baphomet alongside deities may be controversial, but they certainly hold a unique energy which you may wish to explore. Their image was conjured as the manifest representation of the union and balance of all that is, and as such, they know how to turn tension and division into strength and power.

Symbolism and Imagery

A Baphomet image
Goat or goat skull/horns
The phrase "solve et coagula"
An inverted pentagram (a five pointed star with two points upward)

A Working; The Alchemy of Union with Baphomet

Before the ritual spend some time journaling or in contemplation of the thoughts and feelings within yourself around your own sexual nature. Are there any roles you play in your life which you feel mean that you cannot also be a sexually whole being? Pinpoint a role you hold which is important to you but which seems like if you are this, you cannot also be a red witch. Perhaps this role is "respectable worker", "dutiful child", "upstanding citizen", "feminist", "spiritual person", "parent", or something else.

You may also choose to work with more abstract perceived duality such as above/below, dark/light, male/female, hot/cold, fire/ice, and so on, or with other aspects of yourself. If possible, using three candles on your altar can work well for this.

~ Prepare yourself and your space for ritual.

~ Perform the ritual opening of your choosing and place an offering to Baphomet on your altar.

~ Invite Baphomet to witness and support your work.

~ Sit with them for a while, allow them to communicate with you.

~ When you are ready, imagine you are holding your nature as a healthy sexual being in your left hand. Really feel its weight and presence. Feel what it means to you. What energy does it carry?

~ Once you have a strong sense of the first part, light the left hand candle.

~ Now, in your right hand, do the same for the other role you have identified as important but contradictory to being your whole sexual self. Once you have a strong sense of this role, light the right hand candle.

~ Sit with these two roles, feeling the tension between them.

~ If it is safe to do so, take the left candle in your left hand and the right candle in your right hand.

~ Imagine each flame carrying those energies for you.

~ Bring them together and light the central candle with both flames at once, allowing yourself to recognise that you are bigger than either role and can be both a red witch and all the other roles you choose to take on in your life.

~ Contemplate the nature of Baphomet, who holds apparent contradictions together in one being whilst still being themselves. Consider the ways in which you do this too.

~ Spend as long as you like here, you may choose to do

some divination, to read one of their stories, or to just meditate with them until it is time to close.

~ Thank Baphomet and perform your ritual closing.

~ Make any notes you need to and ground yourself by doing something mundane.

Continue to build your relationship with them over time with prayers, maintaining a shrine, making offerings, and by striving to find the third option between the things that feel divided in yourself.

Babalon

In one way ancient, as she is mentioned in the Bible as the fallen "Babylon the Great" (Revelations, 17:5), Babalon as we know her is a relatively recent Goddess, reborn within Occultism through Thelema. With its emphasis on discovering one's own True Will, Thelema lent that energy to Babalon, who is also called the Scarlet Woman, The Mother of Abominations, or The Red Goddess. Babalon is seen as filled with both lust and power, whole unto herself, seeking pleasure for its own sake, and is depicted as the Strength card in the Thoth tarot deck, renamed "Lust", where she can be seen riding "the beast" and holding aloft the "Holy Grail aflame with love and death". Babalon is seen as epitomising sexual liberation, embodying the Great Mother principle, and expressing the dancing spirit of lust that calls all magicians to rebirth.

Symbolism and Imagery

Red hair or veil
A naked woman riding a beast
Red wine
Lion
Chalice
Septagram (seven pointed star)

A Working; Seeking Ecstasy with Babalon

Dress in something red and comfortable and ensure that any sex toys you like to use are within reach. Choose a drink you particularly like, alcoholic if possible, or as rich and sweet as works for you.

~ Prepare yourself and your space for ritual.
~ Perform the ritual opening of your choosing and place an offering to Babalon on your altar.
~ Call to Babalon and invite her to your ritual, to join you in reaching ecstasy.
~ Pour yourself a drink and hold it aloft, asking her to bless it for you and share in the pleasure with you.
~ Drink and make love to yourself in her honour.
~ Allow yourself to let go as much as you can, a tipsy orgasm, or several, is perfect, as is exploring pleasure in your favourite ways.
~ Spend as long as you like here, you may choose to do some divination, to continue to drink and make love to yourself, or to just meditate with her until it is time to close.
~ Thank Babalon and perform your ritual closing.
~ Leave a glass of drink at her shrine in her honour.
~ Make any notes you need to and ground yourself by cleaning up and doing something mundane.

You can continue to build relationship with Babalon with regular offerings of incense, wine, prayer, and shrine maintenance, or orgasms and ecstatic dancing. Asking her to bless a piece of red jewellery and wearing it out dancing in her honour is a fun option if that is something you are comfortable with.

Star Goddess

The Star Goddess, or God Herself, is found in the Anderson Feri tradition. They are described as "Goddess" to invoke their nature as giving birth to all life through love via the Mother archetype, but also as pre-gender, containing all possibility and so containing all potential sexes and genders. They are the ground of existence, the curved black mirror and starlight of space in which we are cradled. It is said that, before time began, they caught sight of themselves reflected in the blackness of space and fell in love. They made love to themselves and, in the explosion of ecstasy that ensued, all beings were brought into existence from their pleasure and desire.

Symbolism and Imagery

The night sky
Stars
Hearts
A black mirror
A bowl or goblet filled with inky water

A Working; Universal Love with the Star Goddess

If you have a black mirror, or a black bowl you can put water in, place it upon your altar behind a candle (real or LED) so that when it is lit, the light will be reflected in the darkness.

~ Prepare yourself and your space for ritual.
~ Perform the ritual opening of your choosing and place an offering to The Star Goddess on your altar.
~ Invite them to join you in your ritual.
~ Gaze upon your reflection, whether visually or energetically, and imagine falling in love with the person that you see there. We are each a part of the Divine

Starlight made flesh, pieces of pleasure and desire moving through the world. In this moment, allow yourself to feel that truth.

~ Light the candle and notice the energy and image change.
~ *Recognise* yourself as part of the Divine.
~ Feel the Star Goddess surround you with love.
~ Rest awhile in their arms, in this love.
~ Spend as long as you like here, you may choose to do some divination, to write them love poetry, or to just meditate with them until it is time to close.
~ Thank The Star Goddess and perform your ritual closing.
~ Make any notes you need to and ground yourself by doing something mundane.

You can continue to build relationship with them by maintaining a shrine, tuning into their love regularly, stargazing, making offerings, composing love poetry, and any other options which reveal themselves to you.

Self-Love Check-In

How are you feeling? Has anything excited or unsettled you in this chapter? What might that tell you about yourself? Which deities appeal to you now, if any? What does the imagery and symbolism tell you about them? About yourself? How are you feeling about the idea of working with deities at all? If you have tried any of the workings, how has that gone? Are there any workings or deities that you feel like you will never engage with? What does this tell you about yourself?

Remember that you get to choose. Take some time now to remind yourself that you choose love and self-care by returning to the familiar self-love check-in practice.

Take a few minutes to check in with yourself and make a list of three things, as we did in the previous chapters.

1. What do you need right now?
2. What do you desire?
3. What are you grateful for?

Go and do at least one thing you need and one thing you desire. Remember that you are deserving of love and pleasure.

Part V
Underworld Magic

Chapter 12

Kink, BDSM, and Facing Taboos

The Taboo of the Dungeon

And so Inanna descended into the Underworld, through seven gates which, one by one stripped away her worldly power. Once there she was flogged and hung upon a hook as if dead. But, after her return, she was more powerful than before for she had faced death, naked and alone, and been reborn.

The mere mention of sex in itself is enough for many people to blush and turn away, and to expand the topic out to sacred sex, or even (horror of horrors!) sex magic, is to invoke two taboos at once. Three taboos, in fact, as the very idea of considering sex to be spiritual, and the spiritual to be sexy, is another layer all of its own. But once we move past this cultural discomfort, we start to accept that there is healing to be found where *eros* dances.

And then we may encounter another challenge. It is often enough that we are choosing to embrace our sexual selves, but because so much of both sex and magic are considered unsuitable for discussion in "polite society", those aspects of our sexuality which do not fit within the tidy boxes considered standard are taboo even for outsiders who dare to engage with both magic and their nature as sexual beings.

I am, here, talking about kink. If you already know that this is a topic which you are unsettled by then please feel free to leave this chapter entirely. If you choose to read on, I will not be sharing any practical exercises in this chapter but I invite you to consider the contents and note down any thoughts or feelings that arise as you read. I am including it because this is an important part of many people's sex lives, and I have personally met many people for whom kink and BDSM have played a hugely healing role in their lives. This chapter is an offering to the fearless deities of passion and those that found wholeness in the dungeon, in the hopes that it will help dispel a misunderstanding or two and suggest why this path may be important to some.

No one act or path is right for everyone, but as the Goddess says; all acts of love and pleasure are, indeed, sacred.

What is Kink and BDSM?

And Lilith refused to lay underneath Adam the way he said she was supposed to. Instead, she chose freedom, and pleasure on her terms. Some people say she birthed all the monsters of the world, perhaps they were just jealous that she did what they never could... accepted herself.

Kinks are those desires, those turn-ons that are considered non-standard. They are activities and objects which are pleasurable in unexpected ways. And because they are considered weird if we have certain kinks, we may find ourselves scared to engage with our own desires. We may struggle to accept them in ourselves, or fear others finding out, even when they are entirely harmless. Accepting our full selves, including our kinks, is part of embracing the entirety of our healthy sexuality.

BDSM overlaps with kink, and refers to the people and communities that meet under the labels of "Bondage and Discipline, Domination and Submission, Sadism and Masochism", and often those folk who are connected to them. These things are not always sexual, but our focus here is on that part of them which is linked in with our nature as pleasure-seeking, embodied, magical beings. Ultimately it serves no one to resign parts of our beings to the shadows, and yet some parts of ourselves do best in the dungeon. Which is a poetic way of saying that the path of kink and the path of spirit are, for many, the same.

In kink and BDSM, consent is central. Clear, freely given, informed consent. When we accept all of what we are, we accept who we love, where we find pleasure, and what turns us on, and meet with others who choose to share in that with us, then we find healing too. Within the magic circle has long been a place to break the cultural taboos that keep us from our power, which includes being comfortable with our sexual selves.

Within kink the aspects of our sexual selves which we keep in the shadows can be explored and accepted within relative safety. Fantasy, roleplay, explorations of power, and sensory exploration are all tools which can be used to open the possibility for healthy, whole, expressions of our selves.

The methods used in BDSM can also be useful in ritual and magic. Blindfolds and sensory deprivation may be a turn-on, and also heighten trance and magical perceptions. Sensory play and careful explorations of sensations such as pain have long been known as routes into ecstatic trance, or as ordeals and ritual challenges.

For some, these things are part of their desires, and within communities which use them there are structures of negotiation, consent, and education on minimising risks. For others, these are tools they use to travel between the worlds and touch the divine.

In both cases, if this is a path that calls you then know that it will break down barriers within yourself, because denying parts of yourself only cuts you off from your potential, but fully accepting yourself reconnects you to your power. Kinky spaces also can provide a safe place in which to explore dressing in different ways, and discussing sexual topics relatively openly. For many people, exhibitionism, voyeurism, or simply being allowed to be sexual can be their whole kink! So simply dressing up and being around others who are doing so can be massively healing. Different venues and events have different rules and atmospheres, so choose according to your preferences.

And if this is not a path that calls you, then know that you do not have to walk it. If this is not a part of you, then you are denying nothing by walking the other way and allowing others the space to be their whole selves.

There are many different parts to BDSM and kink, however, so allow me to highlight just a few pieces of the puzzle below.

Negotiation and Consent

And so Frey did as Gerda had requested, and gave to her family his magical sword. This was what she'd asked for, what she needed, to know that it would never be turned upon her or those she loved. And he gladly gave it. And of all the gods, they are the pair that remain the most faithful, for a union built on love, trust, and communication is powerful indeed.

Sexuality is such an important, but sensitive aspect of our selves that it pays to consider the environment in which you are expressing it, especially when you are exploring different aspects that you have kept hidden from your usual life. This can be anything including explorations of gender expression, the communication of desire, certain forms of clothing or nudity, or playful roleplay. Simply acknowledging that you are a sexual being can be uncomfortable enough. And depending on what you are exploring, you may need to have the consent of others around you before you do so. Nudity for example, is illegal in some places, inappropriate in others, and unwanted in still more. A kink event can be a safe space in which such exploration and expression is expected, encouraged, and acceptable, depending on the venue. Or you may prefer a nudist retreat.

There is also importance placed on communication and consent, often through negotiation. Negotiation with the people around you is important to ensure that you and they are all aware and respectful of boundaries, buttons, and expectations. Through communicating with each other and seeking consent from anyone involved, we work towards healthy integration of our sexual self without shame.

This is important if you're doing explicit kinky activities, and if you are doing magic around and with others. Everyone deserves the chance to choose whether they are engaged in either form of activity, because not everyone wants to. So, if you take any of the pieces we've worked with in this book to a partner, friend, or magical group, discuss the content and intent before engaging with the activity. Likewise, you get to negotiate for your boundaries, needs, and desires with others who are sharing spaces with you. This includes both other human beings, and deities and spirits. For example, you might live somewhere where there is very little privacy, and asking to have time where you are left alone to do your work is communicating your boundaries. Compromising on the time might be part of your negotiation.

Keep in mind, then, the concept of consent. Kink is *always* consensual, if clear, informed consent is not freely given, then the activity ceases to be kink and becomes abuse. As Red Witches, people who hold sex and pleasure as sacred and precious, who are working towards healing and empowerment, and so we always and only engage in our practices within the boundaries of consent.

Trance and Tools

Cernunnos has sat, cross legged, for thousands of years. His antlers pierce the sky like his blade cuts into the hearts of the animals who give their lives to feed us. That which is used to protect can bring pain, and that which brings pain can bring nourishment. He knows both, this horned gods, as he is both predator and prey, hunter and hunted.

Within ritual spaces techniques which are uncomfortable, or

even painful, may be used to induce trance or raise power. In the right contexts, these can also be a source of pleasure for some people. Intense experiences can focus the mind, trigger shifts in brain chemistry and states of consciousness, act as offerings or sacrifices (of comfort, for example) to deities, or be ordeals through which one confronts their shadows or wounds and integrates, heals, or overcomes them.

And if they are part of your personal kink, then finding ways to accept and engage with these safely can be an experience in becoming whole all on its own.

Techniques from this category which have been used within magic and BDSM throughout history include;

~ Bondage and restraint
~ Flogging or scourging
~ Strenuous activity leading to exhaustion
~ Temporary or ritual body piercing
~ Tattooing
~ Blood letting
~ Fasting
~ Sensory deprivation
~ Specific poses such as kneeling for a long time

And so on. Each one of these carries risks and so is best only utilized with appropriate training, and with careful consideration of the risks and legalities in your area, as these things can be illegal even between consenting adults, but you can see that there are a wide variety of ways in which certain kinky activities can be applied to magical situations, and these have often held a sacred role in cultures throughout the world. The intensity of experience can be a gateway to Divine encounters. Engaging with these can also be a method of breaking down the boundaries between self and power as it is unacceptable to be powerful and so using tools which are also culturally unacceptable, and facing the discomfort and risks involved while managing them as much as possible with safety measures and awareness, can be one way to cross that boundary.

Sacred Kink

Divided for the sake of union, the beginning and end of all that was, is, and must be, God Herself dances.

If you have learned the skills required and they work for you, then engaging with kink can be a powerful way to encourage communication between you and your partner/s. Within kink, where consent is key, bondage, power exchange, and the careful application of sensation, discomfort, or pain, are all ways in which someone can seek empowerment by crossing internal taboos and finding freedom from them. It can be used to face your shadows through ordeals or surrender. And if strong sensations, submission or dominance, or surrender and trust, are things that you desire, it can reunite you with parts of yourself that you have shut away.

In relationship, whether romantic or platonic, the tools of communication and negotiation can help you to identify and speak up for your needs, boundaries, and desires, and can facilitate deeper connections and trust.

In visiting kinky events you may find opportunities to explore your desires, but also the potential expression of yourself – the freedom to dress how you choose without judgment or fear and to know that the others around you have that same choice.

And in magic, the techniques and knowledge gained through a study of kink can, if you choose, be applied to shifting consciousness, seeking trance, raising power, and connecting with the divine.

In all these ways, the practice of sacred kink within the path of the Red Witch, can be a tool for healing, empowerment, self-discovery, and delight.

In The Dance

On the dance floor
the Goddess fills me,
rides me hard as I face death
in my flesh
in the knowing that this will one day
be taken from me again.

I dance with Her,
spiralling sinuous serpentine curves
sliding over skin,
flowing between my lips
I breathe Her in
deeper
and ride
higher
on pulsating rhythms
that fill me
and fill me
and fill me
as She glories,
we glory,
in being alive...

Self-Love Check-In

How are you feeling? Has anything excited or unsettled you in this chapter? What might that tell you about yourself? Sacred kink may not be something which calls to you, but hopefully this chapter has highlighted why it may be useful and important to some people. If it does appeal – and you'll know if it does – then there are some suggestions in the further reading appendix to explore the theory further. Do take the time to explore slowly, as there is a wide wild world out there, and not everyone is safe, as you may already have discovered. You have all the time in the world, savour the journey and be as safe as you can.

Regardless of your next steps, take some time now, then, to remind yourself that you choose love and self-care by returning to the familiar self-love check-in practice.

Take a few minutes to check in with yourself and make a list of three things, as we did in the previous chapters.

1. What do you need right now?
2. What do you desire?
3. What are you grateful for?

Go and do at least one thing you need and one thing you desire. Remember that you are deserving of love and pleasure.

Chapter 13

Closing; At the Crossroads

Cinders

To open the gates
is to risk it all.
To kiss the gods is
to sacrifice
all that could be normal.
Life is never the same.
Consumed
by the heat
in the very bones of life.

It's a risky business,
unleashing desire on the world.

The alternative,
though cleaner,
leaves only cinders
in a shell that longs to dance.

And so, my darlings,
kiss life,
and burn bright.

In Closing

And so, we reach the end. Throughout this book you have had the chance to deepen, again and again, your own *eros*, your Divine Erotic power. There have been opportunities to cultivate that power, to heal old wounds, to develop your confidence in your sexual self, and to build skills and techniques for creating magic. You have met, albeit briefly, deities and archetypes who embody these powers and can teach you more, and more deeply, about your potential through your relationship with them. And you have explored what all this means to you.

By now your Grimoire is likely dripping with magical experiences, thoughts, techniques, and inspirations. Your altar has become a home for *eros*, and your ability to perform sexual spellcasting has expanded.

Every step along this path can heal wounds and remove blocks to your own erotic power, allowing you to become more strongly integrated, so that magic becomes more natural to you, and the magical energy can flow more strongly, boosting the results of spells that you do. The way in which you move through the world may be changing, allowing your inner love and pleasure to shine out, and your whole nature as a sexual being to strengthen your confidence. As a result, the world will respond. The Universe recognises when you shift things and will begin to treat you as the powerful being that you are.

This may unsettle people who are used to you being smaller, wounded, and less confident. They may try to keep you the same as you were because change is scary. If you find that happening, you can give people the opportunity to grow with you, but if they do not, I recommend holding onto yourself and, with as much compassion as you can hold for yourself and them, gently spend less time with them in situations where they can treat you badly. You get to choose who you become, and to maintain your boundaries around your needs, wants, and desires. And they too get to consent, or not, to being around the new you, but they don't get a say in who you choose to be.

I can tell you that it is worth it, however, as I have also been through this journey, I have shared with you here. And the life that unfolds, the friendships, relationships, and connections that arrive and blossom are worth so much more than any that try to keep you from being your whole, glorious, gorgeous self.

At any moment you are choosing, choosing to rest, to continue, to heal, celebrate, connect, love, desire, seek pleasure, integrate possibilities, or face your shadows and burn away shame. In all, you honour *eros*.

A Crossroads Ritual

As one last working before this book is over, I'd like to offer you a ritual to integrate the work you've done, and to recognise how far you've come. Keep this for a point when you feel you have reached a transition point in your journey, when you have done what feels like a cycle in the work. You may have worked through everything in the book, or through all of the pieces that call to you right now. When this happens for you will depend on your journey, so I leave the exact timing in your hands. It contains a guided visualisation, which you might choose to record for yourself, to write out prompts for each step on flashcards, or to have the book nearby for reference as you journey. Allow yourself plenty of space at points where you think you'll need it.

A Pre-Ritual Reflection

Take some time beforehand to reflect on everything that you have done on this path so far. Give yourself a chance to recognise what you have achieved and how far you have come in this healing journey. Remember your successes with your spellcasting, or make note of ways in which the world has shifted to acknowledge your growth.

Which pieces that you've learned will you be continuing to

use? How might you continue to integrate them into your life and regular magical or devotional practice?

Consider which steps you might like to take next, if there is anything that you'd like to revisit at this stage, and what you feel is the next important piece of your journey. Read over the ritual and check in with yourself on whether there is anything you need to consider beforehand. You might choose to amend language to fit you better, or to omit, amend, or add in pieces to improve the ritual for you.

Preparation

Gather all your supplies, check that you have enough light to read anything that you will be reading during the ritual. Make sure that any candles are safe.

Have a bath, shower, or wash with the intention of washing away any negative images you have of yourself.

Set up your altar and your space, ensure that you will be warm enough, comfortable, and undisturbed for the duration of the ritual.

The Ritual

Perform your preferred ritual opening to prepare yourself and your space magically. You can use the Foundational Magical Practice from Chapter 5, expanding the power into a sacred circle;

Breathe in. Be aware of your body.
Breathe out. Release tension and relax.
Breathe in. Be aware of the ground.
Breathe out. Send a root of energy into the earth.
Breathe in. Draw up power from the earth into yourself.
With each breath out, send the root deeper.
With each breath in, draw more power up, filling you.
When you are filled with power and rooted deeply...

159

Breathe out. Send a cord up into the heavens.
Breathe in. Draw starlight down into you, blending with the earth
power.
With each breath out, send the cord higher.
With each breath in, draw more power down.
When you are filled with power and connected strongly...
Breathe out. Let the power that fills you expand out into a sphere.
Breathe in. Pull power up from the earth and down from the stars.
Breathe out. As the sphere expands it pushes the etheric dirt from
your self.
Breathe in. Fill with more power.
Breathe out. Let the sphere of power surround you and expand out
into a sphere of protective golden light that surrounds you and your
space, the edges becoming a sacred circle to safely hold you.

Light your candle with an invocation to the Divine Lover;

A breath of bliss, caught upon the tongue,
I welcome you, invite you; Divine Lover, come.
Red Goddess dancing, spinning like the sun,
Wild God and Bright Spirit; come, lovers, come.
Bless my heart, my mind, my skin,
with touch of pleasure welcomed in,
in your honour I begin,
Divine Lover, come!

And rest awhile in their presence, in the energy of Love and
eros. Let the energy wash over you, fill you, and bathe you in
love, healing and wholeness. You may also choose to make an
offering to one or more of the deities of passion who you have
been working with more closely, if that feels right to you, and to
invite their presence at this ritual.

The Journey

- ~ Allow your eyes to close and relax.
- ~ Imagine a mist rising around you and carrying you down into the inner realm.
- ~ When the mists clear you find yourself stood at a crossroads, where three paths meet, surrounded by a thick, soft, fog. It is night and overhead you can just about see stars through the cloud.
- ~ Behind you is the path that you have travelled so far.
- ~ Before you, in the centre of the crossroads, is a small altar with a cloaked, hooded figure standing behind it.
- ~ On the altar is a bowl of liquid so dark that it seem like the night sky made touchable.
- ~ The figure beckons you toward the altar and gestures for you to scry the bowl of night.
- ~ As you gaze into the darkness you see the path that you have travelled to get here, and the gifts and strengths you have won so far.
- ~ The vision in the bowl clears and is replaced with a vision of you.
- ~ You are surrounded by love.
- ~ You are embodied and powerful.
- ~ You have found and deepened your connection to *eros*.
- ~ You are a Red Witch, working the magic of the Crimson Craft.
- ~ Take some time to recognise yourself as the being that you have worked to become. Healed, whole, and in tune with your own Divine Erotic nature.
- ~ When you have soaked in this vision, the figure passes a hand over the bowl and the vision clears.
- ~ You look up and they remove their hood, revealing a beautiful face with deep, dark eyes.
- ~ This is a Devotee of the Divine Erotic, carrying *eros*.

~ They smile at you and you know that they know you as you the powerful being you are.

~ They have a gift for you, a piece of jewellery that carries a reminder of this power.

~ They offer it to you and if you choose to accept, they put it on you and you feel divine love surround you.

~ They produce two cups of something sweet and lovely and offer you one so you can toast together in honour of you and your journey. They are proud of you.

~ You may spend some time with them now.

~ After a little while it is time to move on and they turn with you to the two paths on the other side of the altar.

~ You notice that there are pillars beside the paths with markings. Consider what these markings say to you about the paths ahead. Notice which direction you are drawn toward. Choose one and, when you are ready, begin to travel down it.

~ As you travel an animal, bird, or creature of some kind appears on the path. They will be your guide on the next stage of your journey through the Crimson Craft. Greet them and ask them if there's anything they need to tell you at this stage.

~ The mists begin to rise again from this land and you relax into them, bidding your new guide farewell.

~ You are returned to where you began in your ritual space.

~ Take a moment to ground yourself and, if you choose, spend a little time journaling or doing divination.

The Ritual Closing

When you are ready, thank the divine erotic;

Lovers three I honour you,
Let your blessings flow,
Know that you are welcome here,

and help my magic grow.
Let me know your sacred ways,
Of love and sex divine,
For now I bid you kind farewell,
You to your homes and me to mine.

Breathe into your core for a moment and centre yourself in your body. As you breathe, let the excess power that fills you, any which you do not need, drain away into the earth and sky. Let the sphere of light shrink around you, until you are in your shield, surrounded by light, protected, clean, and energized. Let the connections to earth, sky, and *eros* fade from mind, but know that your root and your cord to the stars are always there, feeding you.

Make any notes in your journal that you feel you would like to remember. Finally, go and do something mundane and grounding, bringing yourself back to everyday consciousness before jumping into the rush of the world if you can.

You may like to make or acquire an item of jewellery to represent the piece the Devotee gave you as your gift upon this path, to keep on your altar and wear during your workings, and a representation of your new guide. Whenever you wish, you may return to the crossroads and meet your guide there to converse or be shown the way ahead.

One final Self-Love Check-In

How are you feeling? How are you feeling about the work in this book that you have done?

Look back over the lists you've made in each chapter. Look at the things that you've noticed you need. Look at the things you've noticed that you desire. Look at the things you have been grateful for.

These can form the basis of a list of things to look over whenever you need support, whenever you are stuck for how to show yourself care. They are also things which you have, hopefully, done and so together can act as a reminder of ways in which you have been good to yourself.

Compile them into one place. Notice if there are any patterns that can tell you something useful about yourself. Allow yourself to be inspired, and see if you can add three things you need, and three things that would make you smile.

Now, put down this book, and go and do one at least thing you need, and the thing you most desire right now. Remember always that you are deserving of love and pleasure.

A Letter From Your Author

Dear Red Witch,

You have come a long way on the path of the Crimson Craft, and there are so many possibilities ahead for you still. I trust that you have been able to recognise the beauty and power that you hold, to tap into that deep well of sexual power which you carry, and to meet the divine *eros* that flows through your heart.

This book is offered as a collection of keys that open doors and gateways to whole worlds of wonder within you, to temples of delight and the homes of wild and gorgeous gods. These keys are yours now to continue using with integrity.

Thank you for facing the challenges that you have faced, and for having the courage to even consider doing this work for yourself. Each one of us who works towards healing the split between flesh and spirit, who honours sex as sacred, and who reclaims our pleasure and selves as powerful, weaves a piece of an enchantment. The enchantment of returning love and *eros* to their rightful place in the world; accessible to everyone.

I am very proud of you.

Finally, I'd like to invite you to come and join the virtual Crimson Coven, where fellow red witches gather to support each other on the journey, share resources and celebrate together. You can find the door to that community by contacting me, or going here: www.crimsoncoven.carrd.co

In *eros* and delight,
  ~Halo
  www.haloquin.net

Appendices

Appendix 1

Ritual Opening and Closing

Pre Ritual Reflection

You may choose to journal on the upcoming ritual, to clarify your intentions and check in with yourself on whether there is anything you need to consider beforehand. You might choose to amend language to fit you better, or to omit, amend, or add in pieces to improve the ritual for you.

Preparation

Gather all your supplies, check that you have enough light to read anything that you will be reading during the ritual. Make sure that any candles are safe.

Have a bath, shower, or wash with the intention of washing away any negative images you have of yourself.

Set up your altar and your space, ensure that you will be warm enough, comfortable, and undisturbed for the duration of the ritual.

The Ritual

Perform your preferred ritual opening to prepare yourself and your space magically. You can use the Foundational Magical Practice from Chapter 5, expanding the power into a sacred circle;

Breathe in. Be aware of your body.
Breathe out. Release tension and relax.
Breathe in. Be aware of the ground.
Breathe out. Send a root of energy into the earth.
Breathe in. Draw up power from the earth into yourself.
With each breath out, send the root deeper.

With each breath in, draw more power up, filling you.
When you are filled with power and rooted deeply...
Breathe out. Send a cord up into the heavens.
Breathe in. Draw starlight down into you, blending with the earth
power.
With each breath out, send the cord higher.
With each breath in, draw more power down.
When you are filled with power and connected strongly...
Breathe out. Let the power that fills you expand out into a sphere.
Breathe in. Pull power up from the earth and down from the stars.
Breathe out. As the sphere expands it pushes the etheric dirt from
your self.
Breathe in. Fill with more power.
Breathe out. Let the sphere of power surround you and expand out
into a sphere of protective golden light that surrounds you and your
space, the edges becoming a sacred circle to safely hold you.

Light your candle with an invocation to the Divine Lover;

A breath of bliss, caught upon the tongue,
I welcome you, invite you; Divine Lover, come.
Red Goddess dancing, spinning like the sun,
Wild God and Bright Spirit; come, lovers, come.
Bless my heart, my mind, my skin,
with touch of pleasure welcomed in,
in your honour I begin,
Divine Lover, come!

And rest awhile in their presence, in the energy of Love and *eros*.
Let the energy wash over you, fill you, and bathe you in love,
healing and wholeness.

[Perform any ritual working at this point. this can be a working
from this book, from other similar paths, written by yourself, or

you can focus on tuning into the powers which support crimson crafting and your path through it, honouring deities, listening to yourself, divination, and so on.]

When you are ready, thank the divine erotic;

Lovers three I honour you,
Let your blessings flow,
Know that you are welcome here,
and help my magic grow.
Let me know your sacred ways,
Of love and sex divine,
For now I bid you kind farewell,
You to your homes and me to mine.

Breathe into your core for a moment and centre yourself in your body. As you breathe, let the excess power that fills you, any which you do not need, drain away into the earth and sky. Let the sphere of light shrink around you, until you are in your shield, surrounded by light, protected, clean, and energized. Let the connections to earth, sky, and *eros* fade from mind, but know that your root and your cord to the stars are always there, feeding you.

Make any notes in your journal that you feel you would like to remember. Finally, go and do something mundane and grounding, bringing yourself back to everyday consciousness before jumping into the rush of the world if you can.

Appendix 2

Further Reading

For a thorough grounding and deepening in modern witchcraft;
Evolutionary Witchcraft, by T. Thorn Coyle (Jeremy P Tarcher, 2005)

For a practical manual on working sex magic in the Western Magickal Tradition;
Modern Sex Magick; Secrets of Erotic Spirituality, by Donald Michael Kraig (Llewellyn Publications, 1998)

For a modern Western Tantric manual on increasing sexual pleasure (safely);
Urban Tantra, by Barbara Carrellas (Ten Speed Press, 2017)

For a guide to healing your own relationship to sex and desire;
Ecstasy is Necessary, by Barbara Carrellas (Hay House Inc., 2012)

For a classic example of mythopoetic explorations of feminine and masculine archetypes;
Women Who Run with the Wolves, by Clarissa Pinkola Estés (Random House, 1996)
Iron John; Men and Masculinity, by Robert Bly (Rider, 2001)

For a workbook on engaging with trans and nonbinary deities;
Hermaphrodeities, by Raven Kaldera (Asphodel Press, 2010)

For an important exploration of sexuality and gender in magical circles today;
Outside the Charmed Circle, by Misha Magdalene (Llewellyn Publications, 2020)

For an exploration of the sacred through Kink;
Sacred Kink, by Lee Harrington (Mystic Productions Press, 2016)

For my poetic exploration of magical kink;
Twisted; Honest Reflections of a Kinky Witch, by Ms Quin (Herbary Books, 2020)

For an exploration of the magic of the Goddesses of Sex through the lens of Babalon;
The Red Goddess, by Peter Grey (Scarlet Imprint, 2007)

For love poetry to the Goddess;
Thorns of the Blood Rose, by Victor Anderson (Harpy Books, 2003)

For online resources and further recommendations:
www.haloquin.net/resources

About Halo Quin

Halo is a lifelong lover of magic. She is a devotee of Freya and the Faery Queen, a lover of the Welsh gods, a storyteller, philosopher, and kinky, sensual witch working to (re)enchant the world. In the crimson craft and through magic, dance, poetry, and rope, Halo seeks to honour *eros* and help heal that old rift between body and spirit.

Halo is a Feri witch who has trained and taught within Reclaiming witchcraft, a member the Order of Bards Ovates and Druids, Bosswitch of the Crimson Coven Collective, creator of The Enchanted Academy (TEA), and co-founder of The Star Club. And you can, of course, find all these things and more at www.haloquin.net.

A Farewell, for now...

Lovers all I honour you,
Let your blessings flow,
Know the gods are welcome here,
and help our magic grow.
Let us know their sacred ways,
Of love and sex divine,
For now I bid you kind farewell,
You to your homes and me to mine.

MOON
BOOKS

PAGANISM & SHAMANISM

What is Paganism? A religion, a spirituality, an alternative belief system, nature worship? You can find support for all these definitions (and many more) in dictionaries, encyclopaedias, and text books of religion, but subscribe to any one and the truth will evade you. Above all Paganism is a creative pursuit, an encounter with reality, an exploration of meaning and an expression of the soul. Druids, Heathens, Wiccans and others, all contribute their insights and literary riches to the Pagan tradition. Moon Books invites you to begin or to deepen your own encounter, right here, right now.

If you have enjoyed this book, why not tell other readers by posting a review on your preferred book site.

Recent bestsellers from Moon Books are:

Journey to the Dark Goddess
How to Return to Your Soul
Jane Meredith
Discover the powerful secrets of the Dark Goddess and
transform your depression, grief and pain into healing
and integration.
Paperback: 978-1-84694-677-6 ebook: 978-1-78099-223-5

Shamanic Reiki
Expanded Ways of Working with Universal Life Force Energy
Llyn Roberts, Robert Levy
Shamanism and Reiki are each powerful ways of healing; together,
their power multiplies. *Shamanic Reiki* introduces techniques to
help healers and Reiki practitioners tap ancient healing wisdom.
Paperback: 978-1-84694-037-8 ebook: 978-1-84694-650-9

Pagan Portals – The Awen Alone
Walking the Path of the Solitary Druid
Joanna van der Hoeven
An introductory guide for the solitary Druid, *The Awen Alone* will
accompany you as you explore, and seek out your own place
within the natural world.
Paperback: 978-1-78279-547-6 ebook: 978-1-78279-546-9

A Kitchen Witch's World of Magical Herbs & Plants
Rachel Patterson
A journey into the magical world of herbs and plants, filled with
magical uses, folklore, history and practical magic. By popular
writer, blogger and kitchen witch, Tansy Firedragon.
Paperback: 978-1-78279-621-3 ebook: 978-1-78279-620-6

Medicine for the Soul
The Complete Book of Shamanic Healing
Ross Heaven
All you will ever need to know about shamanic healing and how to
become your own shaman...
Paperback: 978-1-78099-419-2 ebook: 978-1-78099-420-8

Shaman Pathways – The Druid Shaman
Exploring the Celtic Otherworld
Danu Forest
A practical guide to Celtic shamanism with exercises and
techniques as well as traditional lore for exploring the Celtic
Otherworld.
Paperback: 978-1-78099-615-8 ebook: 978-1-78099-616-5

Traditional Witchcraft for the Woods and Forests
A Witch's Guide to the Woodland with Guided Meditations and
Pathworking
Mélusine Draco
A Witch's guide to walking alone in the woods, with guided
meditations and pathworking.
Paperback: 978-1-84694-803-9 ebook: 978-1-84694-804-6

Wild Earth, Wild Soul
A Manual for an Ecstatic Culture
Bill Pfeiffer
Imagine a nature-based culture so alive and so connected,
spreading like wildfire. This book is the first flame...
Paperback: 978-1-78099-187-0 ebook: 978-1-78099-188-7

Naming the Goddess

Trevor Greenfield

Naming the Goddess is written by over eighty adherents and scholars of Goddess and Goddess Spirituality.

Paperback: 978-1-78279-476-9 ebook: 978-1-78279-475-2

Shapeshifting into Higher Consciousness

Heal and Transform Yourself and Our World with Ancient Shamanic and Modern Methods

Llyn Roberts

Ancient and modern methods that you can use every day to transform yourself and make a positive difference in the world.

Paperback: 978-1-84694-843-5 ebook: 978-1-84694-844-2

Readers of ebooks can buy or view any of these bestsellers by clicking on the live link in the title. Most titles are published in paperback and as an ebook. Paperbacks are available in traditional bookshops. Both print and ebook formats are available online.

Find more titles and sign up to our readers' newsletter at
http://www.johnhuntpublishing.com/paganism
Follow us on Facebook at https://www.facebook.com/MoonBooks
and Twitter at https://twitter.com/MoonBooksJHP